Understanding
THOMAS BERNHARD

UNDERSTANDING MODERN EUROPEAN and LATIN AMERICAN LITERATURE

JAMES HARDIN, *Series Editor*

ADVISORY BOARD

George C. Schoolfield
Yale University

Charles Porter
Yale University

Theodore Ziolkowski
Princeton University

Roberto González-Echevarría
Yale University

Michael Winkler
Rice University

Sara Castro-Klarén
The Johns Hopkins University

Understanding Günter Grass
by Alan Frank Keele

Understanding Graciliano Ramos
by Celso Lemos de Oliveira

Understanding Gabriel García Márquez
by Kathleen McNerney

Understanding Claude Simon
by Ralph Sarkonak

Understanding Mario Vargas Llosa
by Sara Castro-Klarén

Understanding Samuel Beckett
by Alan Astro

Understanding Jean-Paul Sartre
by Philip R. Wood

Understanding Albert Camus
by David R. Ellison

Understanding Max Frisch
by Wulf Koepke

Understanding Erich Maria Remarque
by Hans Wagener

Understanding Elias Canetti
by Richard H. Lawson

Understanding Thomas Bernhard
by Stephen D. Dowden

UNDERSTANDING
THOMAS BERNHARD

STEPHEN D. DOWDEN

UNIVERSITY OF SOUTH CAROLINA PRESS

Copyright © 1991 University of South Carolina

Published in Columbia, South Carolina, by the
University of South Carolina Press

Manufactured in the United States of America

Library of Congress Cataloging-in-Publication Data

Dowden, Stephen D.
    Understanding Thomas Bernhard / Stephen D. Dowden.
      p.   cm. — (Understanding modern European and Latin American
  literature)
    Includes bibliographical references and index.
      ISBN 0–87249–759–3 (alk. paper)
      1. Bernhard, Thomas—Criticism and interpretation. I. Title.
II. Series.
PT2662.E7Z65   1991
838'.91409—dc20   91–11970

For Žena Redrock

CONTENTS

Editor's Preface   ix
Preface   xi
A Note on Translations   xv
Chronology   xvi

Chapter 1:   Introduction   1
Chapter 2:   The Inability to Sleep: *Frost* and *Gargoyles*   11
Chapter 3:   Sacrificial Sisters: *The Lime Works* and *Correction*   29
Chapter 4:   The Spirit of Anarchy: Autobiographical Works   43
Chapter 5:   The Hidden Wound: *Old Masters* and *Auslöschung* (Obliteration)   59
Chapter 6:   Bernhard as Playwright   71

Bibliography   85
Index   97

EDITOR'S PREFACE

Understanding Modern European and Latin American Literature has been planned as a series of guides to the life and writings of prominent modern authors and their most important works. Modern literature makes special demands, and this is particularly true of foreign literature, in which the reader must contend not only with unfamiliar, often arcane artistic conventions and philosophical concepts, but also with the handicap of reading the literature in translation. It is a truism that the nuances of one language can be rendered in another only imperfectly (and this problem is especially acute in fiction), but the fact that the works of European and Latin American writers are situated in a historical and cultural setting quite different from our own can be as great a hindrance to the understanding of these works as the linguistic barrier.

For this reason, the UMELL series will emphasize the sociological and historical backgrounds of the writers treated. The peculiar philosophical and cultural traditions of a given culture may be particularly important for an understanding of certain authors, and these will be taken up in the introductory chapter and also in the discussion of those works to which this information is relevant. Beyond this, the books will treat the specifically literary aspects of the author under discussion and attempt to explain the complexities of contemporary literature lucidly. The books are conceived as introductions to the authors covered, not as comprehensive analyses. Nor do they provide detailed summaries of plot since they are meant to be used in conjunction with the books they treat, not as a substitute for the study of the original works. The purpose of the books is to provide information and judicious literary assessment of the major works in the most compact, readable form. It is our hope that the UMELL series will help to increase our knowledge and understanding of the European and Latin American cultures and will serve to make the literature of those cultures more accessible.

Professor Dowden's *Understanding Thomas Bernhard* is the first book-length study in English to treat Bernhard's literary career in its entirety. Not a long career, unfortunately, but what a fruitful one it was, bringing forth fifteen novels and long narratives, eighteen plays, six autobiographical works, and several volumes of lyric poetry. Bernhard was notoriously dif-

EDITOR'S PREFACE

ficult, notoriously pessimistic, well known for his attacks on revered cultural monuments, such as the venerable Nobel Prize winner Elias Canetti, and political figures, such as Austrian chancellor Bruno Kreisky. But in many ways his works address the fortunes of postwar Austria, a tiny country that has played a supremely important role in the history of twentieth-century European culture. Dowden's clear, intelligent book provides access to a daunting literary oeuvre in which the aesthetic and literary currents of the postwar period are interestingly and significantly reflected.

J. H.

PREFACE

Skeptical intellectuals and pessimistic writers can be irritating. Denis Diderot, the eighteenth-century *philosophe* (and an irritating intellectual in his own right), once offered a few interesting remarks about these difficult characters. "I have no high opinion of such eccentrics," says one of his narrators; "others make companions or even friends of them. They detain me once in a year when I happen to bump into them, because their character stands out against all the rest, and they disrupt the tedious uniformity which our education, our social conventions, and our manners have introduced among us. If one of them turns up in a group of people he is the bit of yeast that leavens the whole and restores to each of us a little of his natural freedom. He stirs things up and gives people a jolt, forces them to take sides, brings out the truth, shows who the really good ones are and unmasks the villains. That's when the wise man listens and sorts people out." Diderot's man is talking about the eccentric title figure of *Rameau's Nephew*. But his comments also touch at the life, personality, and continued literary presence of Thomas Bernhard, Austria's great literary eccentric (and, not coincidentally, the author of a book called *Wittgenstein's Nephew*).

Bernhard liked to think of himself as a *Störenfried:* a troublemaker, an eccentric, a disruptive force in his family, in his native Austria, in the literary establishment. Such people are uncomfortable to live with, but they fulfill a vital need when they inject a little chaos into the regular order of things—especially when they do so in the form of superbly gifted prose. Like the curmudgeons and madmen that populate his books, Bernhard raises hackles by speaking his mind; he calls forth in equal measure both praise and blame; but most of all he generates a welter of images, ideas, and impolite opinions from which the hidden truth can emerge: the truth about his family, his country, the literary establishment, and his other preoccupations.

But the truth is not necessarily what he says it is, or at least not at a one-to-one ratio. The imaginative writer deals in fiction, a species of *untruth* that yields truth only after critical exploration. The truth must be coaxed out of Bernhard's works. My aim in this book is to explore the works of Thomas Bernhard is such a way that their claim on our imagination and on our serious attention becomes clear.

Specifically, my intention in the pages that follow is twofold. First, and most important, I have tried to sketch out for the American audience a picture of Bernhard and his works from the perspective of his Austrian context. Much of his accomplishment becomes visible only when seen through the lens of Austrian history and cultural assumptions. Second, I have tried to make a few preliminary connections between Thomas Bernhard and the literary tradition to which he belongs. My general premise is that Bernhard is primarily a satirist of Swiftian sensibilities. While there is no evidence to suggest that he has been directly influenced by Swift, or any other of the great satirists, Bernhard's achievement is of a similar nature. Recognizing his place in the larger satirical tradition disposes of objections (heard especially in Austria) that Bernhard was a half-crazy crank with an ax to grind. Considering Bernhard's always cantankerous and often vindictive habits of expression, the objection must be taken seriously. But at such a pass one might profitably recall what Flaubert said of his difficult compatriot the Marquis de Sade: "I like such men, these monsters clarify history for me." Bernhard's predilection for scenes of cruelty, vice, and horror make the comparison all the more appropriate.

Bernhard's satirical attacks and horrific visions aim to clarify Austrian history, which he perceives as an unmitigated debacle. Both his vision of history and his idea of literature rest on his uncompromising will to truth. And truth for him is this: a rejection of the comforting illusions of religion, art, and politics. Proceeding from his own experience, he imagines a world in which eccentric figures—especially bitter old men—have learned to live without recourse to metaphysical lies or utopian deceptions. His principal merit as a writer, I think, lies in his willingness to take, at any cost, an articulate stand against the abstractions and alienations that haunt him, and especially those of religion and politics, of art and history. He resolutely insists on knowing (and telling) the truth, no matter how unpleasant it may be.

What underlies the impulse is at bottom a personal moral imperative. This is most obvious in his treatment of his homeland. Bernhard disguises his hatred of human frailty as a hatred of Austria. He takes malicious delight in unmasking the weaknesses and self-deceptions of his countrymen. But in revealing the "truth" about Austria, what he really makes visible is the moral grounding of his pessimism about human nature, about history, and even about art itself.

Apart from placing Bernhard in the satirical tradition, I would like to hazard a general observation on Bernhard scholarship. The besetting problem of Bernhard criticism has been the unfortunate tendency to take Bernhard at his word. He is a chronic name dropper; his books are littered with names like Pascal, Montaigne, Schopenhauer, Wittgenstein, and dozens more. As soon as he tosses off one of the famous names, writers of dissertations and scholarly articles begin to offer contorted arguments in evidence of hidden influences and secret systems. More often they force a foreign system of thought on a highly individual and idiosyncratic *creative writer.*

Though Bernhard was unquestionably a well-read and thoughtful man, he was not a philosopher and did not write his books and plays according to any set of philosophical precepts. It is true that German literature abounds in philosophical novelists (Hermann Broch and Thomas Mann are conspicuous examples), but Thomas Bernhard was not one of them. That he was so interested in a clearly defined set of themes with more or less philosophical overtones is misleading. These themes recur in his books with great insistence, but his approach to them lacks the basic traits of philosophical reflection: impartial detachment, systematic analysis, reasoned critique, a unified and coherent message. Instead, Bernhard's themes are personal and subjective and impassioned. He deals with them imaginatively, even musically, but never analytically. Indeed, he sets them in a fictional context and explores them unsystematically, if not baldly *anti*systematically.

Therefore I do not think it helps much to trace the supposed influence of, say, Wittgenstein or Schopenhauer, to name only two of the various thinkers he implicitly claims as precursors. Bernhard did not rely on a critical method, and he was not trying to illustrate a philosophical system; he was giving form to his personal vision of the world, one which occasionally includes the names of philosophers he happened to read.

Still, we are not relieved of the need to specify Bernhard's place in literary and intellectual history. "The feeling grows," wrote George Steiner some years ago in the *Times Literary Supplement,* "that Thomas Bernhard is now the most concentrated novelist writing in German. His connections . . . with the great constellation of Kafka, Musil and Broch grow ever clearer." Steiner is only partly right: the connections he specifies surely exist, and the feeling is widespread; but Bernhard's relationship to his predecessors is not becoming much clearer. What we need is precisely such clarity about Bernhard's place in the larger scheme of fiction, criticism, and intellectual life.

PREFACE

From this standpoint the more productive approach to interpreting Thomas Bernhard would be to show the concrete links between his best writing and that of his spiritual kinsmen—without regard to the influence question. For example, Steiner places Bernhard in relation to the constellation of Kafka, Broch, and Musil. In the pages that follow I offer brief digressions from this volume's descriptive format in order to show specific lines that connect Bernhard to Kafka, Musil, and Nietzsche (but not to Broch; despite a shared pessimism about history between the two writers, I am inclined to believe that Broch's commitment to religion and myth places him at a considerable remove from the nihilist Bernhard).

The work of such interpretation is necessarily piecemeal. It will take much work by many hands before a reasonably complete image of Bernhard's achievement is formed. My aim in the present book is simply to offer a means whereby the work might proceed in a productive manner. I have made no attempt to carry on a debate with the presently available secondary literature on Bernhard. The literature is already so extensive that a systematic survey of it would result in a long book, and probably a dull one as well. Most of the studies that have appeared on Bernhard are dissertations from West Germany. The essays that have been written are mostly reviews, and those that are not tend to take up highly specialized questions. The three book-length surveys of Bernhard are available only in German and in any case are now several years out of date.

A NOTE ON TRANSLATIONS

Unless otherwise cited in the notes at the end of each chapter, all translations from the German are my own. The titles of Thomas Bernhard's books and plays will be given first in German, followed by the date of German publication, the English translation, and the date of English-language publication (if it has appeared in translation). For example: *Korrektur* (1975; translated as *Correction,* 1979). Subsequent citations of the title will be in English, even when the passages referred to come from the German original.

Books that have not appeared in translation will be cited first by their German title followed by my translation of it and the date of publication in parenthesis. For example: *Auslöschung* (Obliteration, 1986). Subsequent references to untranslated books will be made in German.

CHRONOLOGY

9 or 10 Feb. 1931	Thomas Bernhard is born in a Dutch home for unwed mothers to Herta Freumbichler. The father, Alois Zuckerstätter, has abandoned mother and child.
1931	Bernhard is cared for on a boat in Rotterdam. His mother is employed as a menial.
July 1932	Herta moves with Thomas to Vienna, where her father, Johannes Freumbichler, lives with his mistress, Anna Bernhard (Herta's mother).
Jan. 1935	Thomas moves with his grandparents to Seekirchen, near Henndorf.
Fall 1936	Herta Bernhard marries Emil Fabjan, who never officially adopts Thomas. They remain in Vienna; Thomas remains in Seekirchen.
1937	Thomas and his grandparents are occasional guests in the home of Carl Zuckmayer.
Oct. 1937	Fabjan moves to Traunstein (in Bavaria) to find work.
Jan. 1938	Herta and Thomas move to Traunstein.
15 Apr. 1938	Birth of Hans Peter Fabjan, Bernhard's half-brother.
Nov. 1938	Freumbichler marries Anna Bernhard, after thirty-four years together.
Spring 1939	Bernhard's grandparents move to a village near Traunstein.
1943	Death of Alois Zuckerstätter.
1943–45	Boarding school in Salzburg.
Fall 1945	The Germans deport the Freumbichlers and Fabjans back to Austria.
1946	The families take up residence in Salzburg.
1947	Bernhard gives up school to become a grocer's apprentice.
Feb. 1949	Bernhard is hospitalized with a severe case of pleurisy, then pneumonia.
1949–51	Pneumonia and tuberculosis. Various sojourns in hospitals and convalescent homes.

11 Feb. 1949	Johannes Freumbichler dies in Salzburg.
13 Oct. 1950	Herta Fabjan dies in Salzburg.
Fall 1951	Studies in Vienna at the Hochschule für Musik and darstellende Kunst.
1952–55	Works as a free-lance writer and court reporter for the *Demokratisches Volksblatt,* a socialist newspaper in Salzburg. Writes short cultural pieces for the radio (ORF).
1955–57	Studies at the Mozarteum in Salzburg (drama and music).
1957–60	Association with Gerhard Lampersberg and his circle at Lampersberg's retreat in Carinthia.
1957	*Auf der Erde und in der Hölle* (On Earth and in Hell)
1958	*In hora mortis*; *Unter dem Eisen des Mondes* (Beneath the Iron of the Moon).
1959	*die rosen der einöde* (The Roses of the Wasteland; libretto).
1960	Serves in London as librarian at the Austrian Institute.
1963	*Frost.*
1964	*Amras*; Julius Campe Prize.
1965	Takes up permanent residence at Ohlsdorf, a village near Gmunden in Upper Austria; Literature Prize of the Free Hanseatic City of Bremen.
1967	*Verstörung (Gargoyles)*; *Prosa* (Prose); Literature Prize of the League of German Industry.
1968	*Ungenach*; Austrian State Prize for Literature; Anton Wildgans Prize.
1969	*Watten* (Playing Cards); *Ereignisse* (Events); *An der Baumgrenze* (At the Timberline).
1970	*Ein Fest für Boris* (A Party for Boris); *Das Kalkwerk* (The Lime Works); Büchner Prize.
1971	Reading tour of Yugoslavia; *Gehen* (Walking); *Midland in Stilfs.*
1972	*Der Ignorant und der Wahsinnige* (The Ignoramus and the Madman); Franz Theodor Csokor Prize; Adolf Grimme Prize; Grillparzer Prize.
1974	*Die Jagdgesellschaft (The Hunting Party)*; *Die Macht der Gewohnheit (The Force of Habit)*; Hannover Dramatists Prize; Prix Séguier.
1975	*Der Präsident (The President)*; *Die Ursache (An Indication of the Cause)*; *Korrektur (Correction).*

1976	*Die Berühmten* (The Big Names); *Der Keller* (*The Cellar*); Literature Prize of the Austrian Federal Chamber of Commerce; *Minetti*.
1978	*Immanuel Kant*; *Der Atem* (*Breath*); *Der Stimmenimitator* (The Voice Mimic); *Ja* (Yes).
1979	*Der Weltverbesserer* (The Universal Reformer); *Vor dem Ruhestand* (*Eve of Retirement*); Bernhard withdraws from the German Academy for Language and Literature.
1980	*Die Billigesser* (*The Cheap-Eaters*).
1981	*Die Kälte* (*In the Cold*); *Über allen Gipfeln ist Ruh* (O'er All the Treetops is Repose); *Am Ziel* (The Goal Attained); *Ave Vergil*.
1982	*Ein Kind* (*A Child*); *Beton* (*Concrete*); *Wittgensteins Neffe* (*Wittgenstein's Nephew*); Premio Prato.
1983	*Der Schein trügt* (*Appearances Are Deceiving*); *Der Untergeher* (Going Under); Premio Mondello.
1984	*Holzfällen* (*Woodcutters*); *Der Theatermacher* (*Histrionics*); *Ritter, Dene, Voss*.
1985	*Alte Meister* (*Old Masters*).
1986	*Einfach kompliziert* (Simply Complicated); *Auslöschung* (Obliteration).
1987	*Elisabeth II*.
1988	*Der deutsche Mittagstisch* (The German Lunch Table) *Heldenplatz*; Prix Médicis.
1989	Bernhard dies 12 February at his home in Ohlsdorf; *In der Höhe* (Up High).

Understanding
THOMAS BERNHARD

CHAPTER ONE

Introduction

Bilious, gloomy Thomas Bernhard has come to be known as one of the German language's most challenging and original postwar writers. Between 1963 and his death in 1989 Bernhard published fifteen novels, the best known of which are *Verstörung* (1967; translated as *Gargoyles,* 1970), *Das Kalkwerk* (1970; translated as *The Lime Works,* 1973), and *Korrektur* (1975; translated as *Correction,* 1979). He is also the author of several memoirs and a few volumes of lyric poetry. Few of his eighteen full-length stage plays have been performed in English, perhaps because they are too steeped in the history and culture of Austria, perhaps because they seem too philosophical to suit the taste and tradition of the American or British stage. Bernhard's dramas are conspicuously short on dramatic action, relying on the power of the word to provoke and disturb. Their strength lies in the compelling poetry of his language or, more exactly, in the cunning wreckage of lyric and dramatic language.

Bernhard's literary reputation as both novelist and playwright rests above all on his powerful and unique style. He composed his works in what is usually characterized as a musical idiom. In his novels he favors long, unparagraphed blocks of prose driven by a strong emphasis on the natural cadences of Austria's musical spoken German. The prose hammers at the reader's nerves with the more or less musical device of verbal repetition, and Bernhard's technique of elaborating a few basic themes into many variations also suggests a musically defined talent. The effect of his best monologues, often sustained for dozens of pages, is that of transforming language into an absolute form, like music. Bernhard himself emphasized the musical dimensions of his prose:

> It has much to do with music. Yes, what I write is intelligible if you understand that the musical component takes precedence, and that *what* I write is secondary. Only when that is present can I begin to describe things and events. The problem lies with the *how.* Unfortunately the critics in Germany have no ear for the music that is so essential to the writer. For me the musical element is as satisfying as when I play the cello—in fact, even more so because the thought that is to be expressed is added to the music.[1]

The result of his highly individual technique is a forbidding style fraught with "difficulty" in the tradition of modernist writing.

Yet this uncompromising stylist is also a commercially successful writer, since 1965 a mainstay of West Germany's prestigious Suhrkamp publishing house. Bernhard's *popular* reputation probably rests on his aggressive personal style; he liked to antagonize the prominent and the powerful. His popularity also stems in part from the exotically repulsive things he chose to write about: disease, isolation, madness, and death. The attraction of forbidden topics and outrageous behavior is strong, and Bernhard made the most of both. Even in Austria, a country famous for curmudgeonly intellectuals, Thomas Bernhard stands out as a grand master of contempt and malediction. In his fiction and drama, in speeches and interviews, he tirelessly heaps abuse on the people and themes that preoccupy his literary attention: Austria, European civilization, human nature, doctors, politicians, artists, women, and even himself.

His contentious personal style won him an enthusiastic following and, naturally enough, some angry detractors.[2] But Bernhard seemed to thrive on the controversy he generated. In a vein recalling Swift's contempt for the Irish, or Nietzsche's ridicule of the Germans, Bernhard maligns Austria and the Austrians in elaborate cascades of abuse. The city of Salzburg can serve as a preliminary illustration. It was there that Bernhard spent an adolescence more miserable than most, and consequently his hometown has earned a place of special loathing on his index of Austrian horrors:

> Salzburg is a deceitful façade, a monument to the world's mendacity, behind which creativity and the creative artist are doomed to atrophy, disintegration, and death. This city of my fathers is in reality a terminal disease that its inhabitants contract through heredity or contamination, and if they do not escape at the decisive moment, they sooner or later directly or indirectly under all these dreadful circumstances either kill themselves suddenly or they perish slowly and wretchedly, directly or indirectly, on this at bottom thoroughly and murderously misanthropic architectonic-archdiocesal-feebleminded-nationalsocialist-catholic soil. For anyone who knows the city and its dwellers Salzburg is superficially beautiful, but beneath the surface it is in fact a loathsome cemetery of dreams and desires.

A connoisseur of spite, Bernhard relished hyperbole and confrontation. Nor did he discreetly confine his obloquies to fictional or impersonal generali-

INTRODUCTION

zation. Without discernible provocation he launched vitriolic assaults against public figures, heckling them in defamatory letters to newspapers. He derides Nobel laureate Elias Canetti as a literary has-been impaired by "galloping senility." He denounces Austrian chancellor Bruno Kreisky (at a time when he was still in office) as "an obstinate old idiot who, having become chancellor, is now quite unpredictable, a megalomaniac and a public menace." In his wittier mode he characterizes Kreisky as Austria's *Salzkammergut- und Walzertito,* an acidly funny epithet that defies translation. In short, it is a mean-spirited dig at Kreisky (and Tito) that draws its venom from Austria's long-standing dread of "balkanization."

The list of Bernhard's petty skirmishes could go on at length, and would have.[3] But in February of 1989 the tirade permanently abated. Lifelong heart and lung disease claimed Bernhard at the age of fifty-eight. What remains of his achievement, and what offers lasting appeal to the critical imagination, lies deeper than the sensationalism of his public feuds. Bernhard's writing offers to the attentive skeptic—for only the most skeptical reading of this writer makes sense—a richly imaginative response to the most dire possibilities of human thought and experience.

Bernhard's art is one of satire. His frequent claims to verisimilitude cannot be taken seriously, except as a part of his pose. It is more accurate to describe his fiction and theater as imaginative reflections upon the darkest side of human nature. His satirical assaults work by breaking the spell of routine experience and opening the reader's imagination to possibilities he or she would not ordinarily care to contemplate. Bernhard's musical nightmares dissolve, deform, and re-create the familiar world in such a manner that we suddenly catch a glimpse of what might lie sunken beneath our habitual way of looking at things. In particular, his fiction unearths a moral underworld fraught with the least appetizing human possibilities, a world that has gone out of control.

But a word of caution is in order. The idea of a subterranean world may be misleading if it suggests an imagination schooled in psychoanalytic categories. Bernhard's interior landscape does not spring from the unconscious. Rather, its sources are history and politics, and in particular the moral calamity of Nazism. As Bernhard sees it, Austrian life and spirit (though not only Austrian) have been transformed into a moral wasteland. He depicts the ravaged landscape with relentlessly caustic severity and with all the rhetorical means at his disposal. Satire is Bernhard's fundamental literary mode, and it is meant to awaken the reader to the moral wilderness within.

In keeping with the satiric tradition of Swift, Bernhard is an uncompromising and militantly impractical moralist. He is bent on experimenting with the literary possibilities of expressing his highly individual ethical vision. "Experimentation," reports the narrator of his novel *The Lime Works,* "was all there was, all he cared about, the whole world was an experiment, everything was." The same could be said of Bernhard's approach to writing. In a spirit of investigation he seeks out the most difficult and perverse avenues of experience, the paths of utmost pain and misery. He proceeds by pushing the imagination to its moral, philosophical, and aesthetic limits, and sometimes beyond. His entire oeuvre amounts to one unswerving experiment in thinking against the grain, in forcing the imagination to explore the parts of life it resists the most. This is why the Bernhard protagonist is habitually cantankerous and negative. He thinks not only against the world but also against himself, against his origins, his biological existence, his spiritual essence. The grinding friction of such thinking is what is most important: it generates the spark that fires the moral imagination.

Though abundant, Bernhard's output comprises a mere handful of ideas and themes, and these he explores with dogged tenacity. It is not unfair to say that one single theme preoccupies this most expansive of minimalists. It is the presence of death, paralyzing and incomprehensible, in the midst of life. Death, life's defining reality for Bernhard, cancels all possibility of transcendence. The thematic prominence of death and its opposite, transcendence, may call to mind the literature of existentialism. Nevertheless, his position is not to be confused with the existentialism of Camus, for example. Camus's prototypical antihero, Sisyphus, achieves a moment of inward victory even in total defeat. Tough-minded Bernhard grants his protagonists no such tragic consolation. In its place we find a "comic" insight into the basic human plight, which is the certainty of death. It is comic not because it is funny (even though Bernhard occasionally generates laughter, especially in the plays), but because life is made to seem a grim practical joke. The joke is this: No larger significance—tragic or otherwise—is possible. Comedy arises when people attempt to create meaning or convince themselves that the world holds something for them.

Bernhard regards with skepticism the existentialist premise that man can or should create meaning in an otherwise absurd cosmos. In fact, Bernhard's fiction ridicules the proposition as a flight from truth. And the truth is utter, bleak, absolute hopelessness. The unredeemed absurdity of the cosmos simply offers itself as the setting for his austere comedy of catastrophe, despair, and mockery. Rejecting the pathos of existentialism, Bernhard ponders the fate of his protagonists as they gradually slip into the maw of oblivion.

Oblivion is the wellspring of his stories and plays; it sets his plots into motion, though the word "plot" may be too strong for the scant action they offer. Bernhard resolves death into what might be called the "verbal action" of introspection. (What Bernhard's fiction and drama lack in plot he makes up for in poetry.) The omnipresence of death motivates the protagonist's concerted effort to discover the inner man, his identity and value, his weight when set on the scales against nullity. The weight of the self always turns out to be inconsequential in a way that Milan Kundera, another heir to the pessimist tradition of Central European letters, has formulated memorably as "the unbearable lightness of being." But Bernhard's protagonists probably suffer from the lightness more than do Kundera's. Kundera's melancholy heroes are at least granted a momentary refuge in the pleasures of the flesh. Bernhard's tortured bodies know only isolation, bitterness, and asceticism. Erotic pleasure offers them no respite from the contemplation of death.

Given that the fate of a Bernhard protagonist is sealed and beyond any mitigation, we may reasonably wonder why Bernhard bothers to write at all. Bernhard scorns hope as childish illusion, and his writing offers no promise of personal, political, or social transcendence. He seems driven solely by a need to know the worst, and thus the *need to know* is a preliminary point of reference. Even though the struggle between intellect and death can only end one way, Bernhard—driven by his need—cultivates an observant sympathy with what is at stake in that struggle: identity, will, the self. A characteristically lapidary, slightly comic vignette from his collection of miniatures *Der Stimmenimitator* (The Voice Mimic, 1978) offers a clue to Bernhard's greater undertaking:

> In the Great Hall of the University Library in Salzburg, a librarian hanged himself from the large chandelier because suddenly, he explains in the note he left behind, after twenty-two years of service he could no longer bear to shelve and charge out books that had been written for the purpose of creating misery, by which he meant all books that had ever been written. This recalled to me the brother of my grandfather, who was a forest ranger at Altentann near Henndorf and shot himself on the pinnacle of Mount Zifanken because he could no longer stand human misery. He, too, left his insight behind in a note.

Bernhard's fiction as a whole might profitably be regarded as a collection of suicide notes. Death overtakes the protagonist in the midst of the world most familiar to him—the librarian's reading room or the forest ranger's mountaintop. Bernhard was not a suicide himself, but he died alone in the familiar surroundings of his farmhouse. Death is with us at every ordinary moment, and may strike anywhere. But "the note," literature, remains as a testament to the struggle. When it has managed to leave traces of itself behind, the self has not been utterly annihilated. Consequently, Bernhard's central theme is not so much the futility of life as the struggle against death, no matter how hopeless that struggle may be.

Because dying is never abstract—it is always personal and individual—Bernhard concentrates on the individual's confrontation with the certainty of not being. Individuality, then, emerges as another major theme. Bernhard conceives of the autonomous individual—man in the form that the Enlightenment conceived him—as a species poised on the brink of extinction. Homo austriacus is his case in point, both for the possibility of autonomous self-determination and its opposite, conformist self-deception. He links conformism to Austria's historical embrace of Catholicism and Nazism. The conformists are embodied in the corrupt families who symbolize for Bernhard the decay of Austrian civilization. But they still manage to produce the occasional individualists who are Bernhard's protagonists. They are the Austrian nonconformists, sometimes modeled on true individualists such as Ludwig Wittgenstein, the Canadian pianist Glenn Gould, or Bernhard's own grandfather. The protagonists characteristically stake everything on preserving their intellectual autonomy, but in their zeal they press their claims too far, to the outermost limits of isolation, madness, and suicide.

These men—for they are always male—are eccentrics bent on completing one or another supposedly grand intellectual project: the ultimate study of hearing, of Mendelssohn-Bartholdy, of physiognomy, or designing the perfect house, and on and on. The project itself makes little difference; what counts is the insane *pride* of the protagonist in his destructive pursuit of perfection. Bernhard amplifies pride to a consuming madness. But the madness is a mannered, literary one. Bernhard's irascible misanthropes exist so far outside the pale of ordinary life and thought that clinical categories cannot contain them. Bernhard offers neither a philosophy nor a theology nor a psychology of death—and certainly not a therapeutic cure for anxiety over it. So far outside our ken is the incomprehensibility of our fate that scientific and religious discourse can offer no insight. It is for this reason, presumably, that Bernhard turns to literature. And psychology is beside the point in Bernhard's hyperconscious world because what he aims to capture in his fiction—for the imagination alone can capture it—is the spirit of the conscious intellect as it vies with death for supremacy. His method is to attack all the complacent and conventional assumptions that make life easy for us; in the person of his protagonists he drives negation to the point of self-destruction by testing his heroes and their values against death. Few survive the test, and none is triumphant.

It would be false to suggest that Bernhard glamorizes or mystifies death in a spirit kindred to that of German romanticism. Death is merely his central point of reference. It is not a mystical dimension but a brute fact from which there is no deliverance and in which no transfiguration to some higher state of being is possible. It would be equally false to suppose that his fiction seeks ascendancy over death through authenticity and autonomy, twin virtues that the existentialists linked to the knowledge of death. Far from being absolute values of the human condition, both turn out to be anchored in the uncertain ground of history and in the changeable essence of the human self. In Bernhard's universe autonomy diminishes the self and severs its lines of connection to the larger human community, especially to family and national identity. And even if these ties were intact, it would not make any difference. History, which for Bernhard almost always refers to the end of Austria-Hungary followed by the catastrophe of the Third Reich, has already debased the Austrian national identity. Authenticity would mean rootedness in that blighted history, which for Bernhard is a morally intolerable identity. In short, autonomy and authenticity do not redeem the individual; they crush him.

The vision of modernity is bleak thus far, but it becomes even darker. For unlike the pessimists who preceded him (Musil, Broch, Nietzsche, Spengler), Bernhard offers no promise of new values to replace the ones he repudiates. He openly welcomes apocalypse, anarchy, and nihilism. However, it would be unduly hasty to accept appearances uncritically. There are at least three essential points that distinguish Bernhard's pessimism from ordinary, shabby cynicism.

First, Bernhard's inexhaustible rancor is that of an outraged moralist. His pessimism springs from the unspoken moral assumptions—internalized vestiges, perhaps, of his Catholic childhood—that give his fiction its ethical drive. It seems likely that Bernhard's contempt for his fellow man disguises a profoundly felt disillusionment with human nature. Grasping this irony is central to understanding Thomas Bernhard. His bitterness gives the measure of severely disappointed expectations and impossibly demanding claims on human nature.

In addition, the absence of compassion and sentimentality from his best work forces the reader or theatergoer into a productive opposition to him, a position that might best be described as a position of "dialectical refusal." By shocking us, Bernhard virtually insists that we test his vision against our own experience and wishes. Bernhard can seldom pass the test; few people's lives are as degraded and miserable as those he imagines. Yet his vision remains strangely compelling. The reason for this lies in the utter coldness of his unsentimental animadversions. Indeed, the inner strength of his writing is predicated on the complete absence of sentimentality. Relentless unsentimentalism, and even cruelty in some instances, has a paradoxical humanizing effect that Kafka explored long before Bernhard was born. "We need books," explained Kafka to a friend, "that affect us like a bad accident. . . . A book has to be the ax that breaks up the frozen sea within us."[4] The hard edges of Bernhard's pessimism block sympathy and encourage reasoned reflection in its place. He demands resistance and skepticism. To agree with Bernhard is to misunderstand him.

The second standpoint from which we can advance critically on Bernhard's nihilism is biographical. The story of his life speaks plainly of a passionate will to live. He was born on 9 or 10 February (Bernhard was not sure) 1931 to Herta Bernhard in a Dutch home for unwed mothers. She had left her native village of Henndorf, near Salzburg, in order to escape the disgrace of bearing an illegitimate child. The father, a carpenter named Alois Zuckerstätter, was later killed in unsavory circumstances in World War II. Bernhard never met him, and Zuckerstätter never acknowledged the child as his son. After two years in the Netherlands, Herta Bernhard returned to Austria and married, but the Great Depression made life extremely difficult for her and her impoverished family. To make matters worse, life with her son Thomas was not easy. By his own account Thomas Bernhard was an unruly boy, and eventually his family exiled him for some months to a distant home for maladjusted children. There his uncontrollable bedwetting brought him much ridicule and torment.

During his early teens in Salzburg boarding school did not suit his nature either, and he eagerly apprenticed himself at the age of fifteen to a grocer in one of Salzburg's more unpleasant postwar districts. Though he enjoyed his menial work there, poor nutrition and hard work finally broke his health. In 1949 the doctors announced to eighteen-year-old Bernhard that he would

INTRODUCTION

soon die of pneumonia, whereupon they committed him to a ghoulish ward reserved for terminal cases. By dint of his will power, Bernhard clung to life and (unlike the typical Bernhard protagonist) successfully struggled toward recovery, even though his initial pneumonia gave way to tuberculosis. To make a desperate situation even worse, as he was battling for his own life, he was in the process of losing his mother to cancer. She died in 1950, not long after her father, Thomas Bernhard's beloved grandfather—a regional novelist popular in the Salzburg area—had also died miserably in a squalid postwar clinic. In spite of these damaging blows to his spirit, Bernhard survived. He never truly regained his health, and seemed to live out of a contempt for death as much as anything. This kind of determination, which Bernhard justly celebrates in his memoirs, is foreign to true nihilism.

Finally, there is a third perspective that helps to illuminate Bernhard's way of writing. He reports in his memoirs that literature and music were instrumental to his struggle against lung disease. That he later chose to become a writer is telling. It is as if Bernhard consciously chose writing as a way to continue his struggle against disease and death. At the same time, though, he remained a confirmed pessimist throughout his adult life, actively denying literature and philosophy as the instruments of transcendence. It is here that the crucial question arises.

If death annuls all meaning in life, including the meaning of art and literature, then what is the status of Bernhard's own literary works? Death sweeps away the claims of even art and literature, as Bernhard seems eager to demonstrate. The artistic protagonist of *Amras* jumps out a window, as does the philosophical one in *Heldenplatz*. The main character of *Frost* destroys all his paintings and becomes a hermit. In *Gargoyles* Prince Saurau's father, also a suicide, found no rescue in Schopenhauer's aesthetic philosophy. "Whatever a human being has done, whatever he has thought," says the protagonist of *Watten* (Playing Cards, 1969), "he should annihilate it." But Bernhard did not follow his own Virgilian advice, if it really was his own advice. Furthermore, even the darkest moments in his works are contradicted by the sheer exuberance of his verbal performance. The vigor of his musical prose, the unmistakable delight in words for their own sake, and the dyspeptic genius of his irony all militate against the outward nihilism that he propounds. Bernhard's more philosophically oriented interpreters sense a need to reconcile the contradiction, to turn Bernhard's thought into a self-consistent intellectual project. But the paradox does not need to be resolved. The inner tension between *what* Bernhard says and *how* he says it is central. It imparts to his writings an ambiguity that is crucial to any imaginative achievement of consequence.

NOTES

1. "Aveux et paradoxes de Thomas Bernhard," *Le Monde*, 7 January 1983: 15.
2. For example, Franz Schuh, "Unterganghofer: Thomas Bernhard in Anekdote und Selbstzeugnis," *salz* 1, no. 2 (1975): 8; Ria Endres, *Am Ende angekommen: Dargestellt am wahnhaften Dunkel der Männerporträts des Thomas Bernhard* (Frankfurt am Main: Fischer, 1980); Lutz Löwengrein, "Thomas Bernhards Seelenschaum," *Forum* (Vienna) 411/412, 11 March 1988: 42-47; Robert Menasse, "Bernhard, Handke & Cie.: Zur Ästhetik der Sozialpartnerschaft," *Forum* (Vienna) Jan./Feb., 1988, 23-25; "*Heldenplatz*-Skandal: Stille Post," *Wochenpresse* (Vienna), 20 Jan. 1989: 43f.
3. Wendelin Schmidt-Dengler, "Bernhards Scheltreden," *Der Übertreibungskünstler: Studien zu Thomas Bernhard*, 2d rev. ed. (Vienna: Sonderzahl, 1989) 93-106.
4. Franz Kafka, *Briefe 1902–1924*, edited by Max Brod (Frankfurt am Main: Fischer, 1975) 27-28.

CHAPTER TWO

The Inability to Sleep: *Frost* and *Gargoyles*

When Austria emerged from the Nazi era in the spring of 1945, most of its important writers were either dead or in exile. Robert Musil had died in Switzerland during the war; Joseph Roth and Ernst Weiβ both died miserably in France, the latter by suicide shortly before the Germans entered Paris and the former of alcoholism; Stefan Zweig committed suicide in Brazil, together with his wife. Hermann Broch and Franz Werfel spent their few remaining years in the United States; Paul Celan settled in France; Elias Canetti chose England, as did the Hungarian Austrian writer Arthur Koestler. Jura Soyfer perished in Buchenwald.

With the better part of its elder generation lost to war, exile, and the concentration camps, Austria's orphaned literary culture found itself in a position to reinvent its tradition. Other parts of the German world responded to the same set of circumstances. West German literature of the era focused its imagination largely on social and political issues. The trend that began with Gruppe 47 after the war only gained in momentum and intensity during the politically tumultuous 60s. Austria did not produce figures comparable in vision to Günter Grass or Heinrich Böll. In the German Democratic Republic, Bertolt Brecht dominated the literary scene. Though he was officially a citizen of Austria, his literature of political advocacy was not of decisive influence there.

The collapse of Nazi Austria in 1945 was followed by years of occupation and ultimately by the founding of the neutral and independent Second Republic of Austria in 1955. The Allies' Moscow Declaration of 1943, for better or for worse, had declared Austria to be the first victim of Nazi Germany. From the perspective of postwar Austria the Allied declaration meant that the burden of historical guilt was to be borne by "the Germans," meaning West Germany; and it meant that the Austrians could set about the business of reclaiming for themselves their own indigenous (i.e., pre-Nazi) history and identity. Consequently, restoring the symbols of national culture was a high priority of postwar Austria. The State Opera reopened in

November of 1955 with a work of Viennese classicism: its performance of Beethoven's *Fidelio* symbolized the renewal of an Austria whose identity was above all cultural.

But opera was not the only cultural front. The federal government energetically pursued a policy of support for the arts on a wider scale by subsidizing orchestras, theaters, museums, artists, and writers. The centrality of high culture in Austrian society (at a per capita expenditure well in excess of even Sweden, France, and the Federal Republic of Germany) has served to inculcate in the Second Republic a national identity that emphasizes the defining force of cultural tradition.[1] Even in foreign eyes Austria's identity has had more to do with art, opera, and museums than with its recent political history. It is hardly an exaggeration to say that the Austrian authorities have successfully exploited Mozart, Beethoven, and Johann Strauss as agents of contemporary foreign policy. With some justification contemporary Austria has been called a theme park of highbrow tourist attractions: the State Opera, the Vienna Philharmonic Orchestra, the Vienna Boys' Choir, the Spanish Riding Academy, the Salzburg Festival, the Art History Museum, and the various state-supported theaters and orchestras. As a result, the popular image of Austria as an apolitical nation of music festivals, art museums, and ski resorts has all but eclipsed its political history. Or at least it had until 1986 when the Waldheim Affair concentrated damaging attention on the official Austrian attitude toward history.[2]

Unlike music, art, and skiing, literature is by nature a more narrowly focused national matter. Within Austria fiction and drama have been an important path of national self-definition. Wary of political entanglements and eager to distance itself from the burden of history, and in marked contrast to West Germany, Austria's cultural establishment did not emphasize literature as a way of reckoning directly with social and political issues. Instead, two basic trends prevailed, one of which aimed to restore to Austria a sense of continuity with its native (pre-Nazi) cultural tradition, while the other resumed the experimental modernism that the Nazi era had interrupted. Neither of the two exhorted its practitioners to transform literature into an instrument of social advocacy or political engagement.

In their support of literature during the 1950s the Austrian authorities favored writers who conformed to the predilections of official culture and prevailing taste.[3] But even with minimal bureaucratic support Austria produced a lively avant-garde scene, embodied during the 50s by the so-called Wiener Gruppe (Viennese Group). During the 60s the center of gravity shifted toward the provincial city of Graz, and the writers who emerged from its controversial arts festival known as Styrian Autumn, from the Grazer Autorenversammlung (Graz Writer's Collective), and from the avant-garde journal *manuskripte*. The best-known writer among those of the 60s is no doubt Peter Handke, who began his career as a writer in Graz. The other outstanding representative of the 60s generation is Thomas Bernhard, who began his career as an outsider from Salzburg, and remained fiercely independent of groups and schools of thought throughout his writing career.

Though fundamentally different in style and temperament, Handke and Bernhard both emerged from the aesthetic atmosphere of Austria during the 50s. The lively modernism debate of the period centered especially on the place of surrealism in postwar writing.[4] Given Austria's historical circumstances, the special appeal of surrealism is not difficult to explain. Within living memory the borders and politics of Austria had undergone changes so radical that they offered little in the way of a stable identity to modern residents. Austria became more an idea than a place. The collapse of the Habsburg monarchy in 1918 was deeply traumatic in itself, but it was an apocalypse that merely presaged yet two more debacles: the failure of the First Austrian Republic followed by the eight years of criminal horror in Hitler's Thousand Year Reich. According to Bernhard, they are failures from which his country never recovered, chances for renewal that Austria let slip away: "The destruction of the monarchy a half a century ago, the destruction of the Third Reich twenty years ago: we have squandered the opportunities!"[5] Austria's historical experience during the first half of the twentieth century only reinforced the traditionally Austrian assumption that the essence of the human condition is its fragility and ephemerality. Under such circumstances the turn to dream, to the alogical, and to an aesthetic of inwardness should be understood as the reach of the imagination for a deeper, more substantial reality than history and politics can offer.

Even before the model of surrealism presented itself, Austria had a strong native tradition of aesthetic inwardness. It reaches back beyond the modernism of Kafka, Musil, Broch, and Rilke, through the classicism of Hofmannsthal and Grillparzer, into the Catholic otherworldliness of the Austrian baroque era. Postwar Austrian surrealism, if it can properly be so called, belongs to the long Austrian tradition of skepticism about the permanence of worldly things. Skeptical of politics, the Austrian literary mind is skeptical too of political literature and of writers who espouse an ideological cause. At a more fundamental level the avant-garde imagination doubts the fixity of outward reality itself because it is constantly exposed to the erosive winds of history, politics, religion, and the epistemological skepticism of philosophers and physicists.

And with the fixity of the world in doubt, the relationship between word and world also falls into ambiguity. Since the great Austrian language critics—Fritz Mauthner, Karl Kraus, and Ludwig Wittgenstein—the tradition of progressive writing in Austria has been centrally informed by *Sprachskepsis,* or the skepticism about how words are able, if at all, to embody without falsity knowledge of the world. For the Austrian avant-garde writer, the flux of language—its historical changes, its endless mutations in metaphor, its moral ambiguity—is the mutable stuff of which reality is constructed. It is the task of literature to explore, dismantle, and reconstruct language in its infinitely complex, and often humorous, relationship to life.

Thomas Bernhard belongs to the tradition of Austrian writing that regards the world and its languages with deep mistrust. "Language is useless when it comes to conveying the truth," he says in his memoirs; "it permits the writer only an approximation, always only a despairing and therefore dubious approximation of its object; language reflects only a falsified authenticity, one that is dreadfully contorted; no matter how much the writer works at it, words flatten everything out, change everything around, and make the total truth into a lie on paper."[6] This view of language underlies Bernhard's idea of literary art.

Though the general drift of his aesthetic proclivities is plain enough, the specific course of his intellectual development remains unclear. Not a great deal is known about his literary associations during the 50s. In the early part of the decade he studied voice and acting in Vienna, and then in Salzburg's famous Mozarteum from 1952 to 1957. Through family connections he secured a free-lance reporting job with Salzburg's socialist newspaper, *Das Demokratische Volksblatt.* But when his employers forced him to join the socialist party, unpolitical Bernhard left the paper and began writing short cultural pieces for Radio Austria (ORF). The experience helped him get his early poetry published in 1957 and 1958, but he was in no way an established writer. He reports, too, that he was writing novels in the 50s. "One was called *Peter Goes to Town,* but by the time I got to page 100, Peter had only got as far as the train station, so I quit."[7] Other, shorter works found their way into print. His earliest published prose and lyric poetry suggest that the avant-garde had not yet fired his imagination. Stories such as *Der Schweinehüter* (The Swineherd, 1954), his newspaper pieces, and his lyric poetry gravitate toward sentimentality about Catholicism, the countryside around Salzburg, and clichés about poor-but-honest country folk.[8] Presumably Bernhard was writing in emulation of his maternal grandfather, Johannes Freumbichler, who had been a writer of locally successful novels about peasant life and manners. But by the late 50s surrealist impulses had begun to influence his imagination.[9]

An anecdote from his student days throws some light on his early interest in the avant-garde. Recalling his final examinations in drama at the Mozarteum, Bernhard once reminisced about the formal presentation he was obliged to make before a board of examiners: "Toward satisfying the requirements for graduation I held forth on the great Artaud. But the seventeen members of the academy's board of examiners had never heard the name Artaud."[10] As with all of Bernhard's anecdotes, this one may or may not be true, may or may not be exaggerated. But in either case it serves as a reliable index to his own aesthetic sympathies, and possibly to those of the conservative orthodoxy of the Austrian academy. Whatever the professors' opinion of his topic may have been, they chose to graduate Bernhard in 1957, when he was twenty-six years old.

By then he had published some short prose in Hans Weigel's progressive literary yearbook *Stimmen der Gegenwart* (Voices of the Present), and he would soon bring out three slim volumes of melancholy poetry. He wrote an unsuccessful libretto for the Austrian composer Gerhard Lampersberg, whom he later satirized in the novel *Holzfällen* (1984; translated as *Woodcutters*, 1987).[11] In 1960 he managed to have three short dramatic pieces staged along with another libretto written for the music of Lampersberg.[12] But Bernhard remained unknown until the publication of his novel *Frost* in 1963. The work was an immediate sensation, due at least in part to Carl Zuckmayer's high praise for it in a well-placed review.[13]

Frost

Frost was a daring and successful experiment. Readers of the modernist classics—Conrad's *Heart of Darkness,* Kafka's *The Castle,* or Thomas Mann's *The Magic Mountain*—will instinctively grasp the framework of *Frost*. It recounts twenty-six days of a young man's pilgrimage into the inner realm. The narrator is an advanced medical student, a resident in surgery, who has been asked by his supervisor to travel to the remote village of Weng, deep in the mountainous interior of Styria. There he is to observe and befriend the supervisor's estranged brother, a misanthropic old artist named Strauch. Over the course of the three weeks Strauch vents his spleen to the younger, less experienced man. The result is a gradual chill that settles in on the student's fragile spirit. His daily journal, together with a few letters he composes, make up the substance of the novel.

Strauch is an artist who has incinerated all of his paintings and retired to the comfortless landscape of the interior—his own and Austria's. The reasons for Strauch's flight from family and vocation have to do with his inability to forget death. The knowledge that death is inescapable has debilitated his life. He finds himself unable to accept any of the conventional, civilizing myths of art, religion, law, or politics. His self-imposed exile in Weng represents a defiant embrace of all that remains uncivilized in himself. In short, Strauch will not, or possibly cannot, sublimate his knowledge of death into the usual channels: religion, art, sex, work. Death is his absolute benchmark, his only certainty. He symbolically consummates his rejection of life-sustaining illusion by destroying the paintings that had been his life's work.

Strauch epitomizes the Bernhard protagonist. He is self-absorbed, histrionically pessimistic, and motivated by a deep loathing of culture and self. At the same time he is strangely charismatic because of the powerfully musical language with which he expresses his inner life. The source of the student's fascination with Strauch—and the source of the reader's interest—is not Strauch's philosophical wisdom. His mind is emphatically not philosophical. Though he is deeply introspective and claims to be a devotee of Pascal, he lacks Pascal's detachment and reasoning judgment. Where Pascal shows restraint and intellectual poise, Strauch indiscriminately spews bile and contempt. He is a grotesquely opinionated cynic, as a few samples of his "wisdom" make plain.

On women: "The feminine is by nature treacherous and subversive. Poison for the masculine mind. For mind itself, for the masculine."

On Austria: "Everything here is barbaric kitsch. Yes, the state itself is feebleminded and its people are pathetic."

On philosophy: "Nothing is progressive and nothing is less progressive than philosophy."

On religion: "God is just one big embarrassment."

On the elderly: "Old men are gourmandizers of the devil and old women pluck at heaven's tits [*Himmelszitzenzieherinnen*]."

On public institutions: "I hate the police, the constabulary, the military, even the fire department."

On attorneys: "A lawyer is a tool of the devil."

The satiric force of his buffoonery is unmistakable. It encourages a comic view of Strauch, even though he is not in general a funny fellow. Bernhard's satire, in *Frost* as elsewhere, does not call forth gales of laughter. It is a comedy of horrors, of human pain unreconciled through the healing mirth that was available to Cervantes and Rabelais, that was still available even to James Joyce, to Hašek, and to the Marx brothers.

Of course satire does not have to be funny. The fourth journey of Swift's Gulliver to visit the Yahoos and Twain's *Mysterious Stranger* are strong witnesses to the grimmer tradition of satire. Bernhard's Swiftian bitterness denounces as sham the utopian dimension implied by the laughter of the great comedians. In his grotesquely satirical world only schadenfreude survives as a last vestige of true merriment. By way of illustration, one need only point to the monstrous tastelessness of Bernhard's first major dramatic piece. His farce of 1968 entitled *Ein Fest für Boris* (A Party for Boris) is peopled with demented paraplegics, monsters rolling around the stage in wheelchairs. The macabre spectacle is comic in a formal sense—intended as a parody of the modern condition—but there is not much to laugh at.

By comparison Strauch seems almost jolly. His comic spirit resides in the supremely self-confident certainty of his anarchical vision. But because anarchy and certainty are incompatible, his hard-won certainty is, comically, worth nothing at all. He is the butt of Bernhard's irony. Still, *Frost* occasionally swerves near the verge of humor. Some of Strauch's views are benignly comic, even sensible (his hatred of lawyers), but the humor is always undone by the other views that are simply malignant (his misogyny). Yet even here there may be a comic edge. Misogyny and misanthropy go, as it were, hand in hand. A true misanthrope would hardly balk at misogyny. Bernhard despises everyone equally.

Attacks on Bernhard for his apparent misogyny, his cynicism, and his downright contempt for the human spirit all miss the larger significance of his imaginative achievement. Concerning Bernhard's treatment of women, which I believe remains insufficiently understood, more will be said in the next chapter. For now, suffice it to say that Bernhard's readers are ill-advised to accept any individual part of Strauch's "philosophy" at face value. What should arrest our attention instead is the effect of the novel as a whole, as an aesthetically and historically conditioned artifact. "A work of art," observes Theodor Adorno, "only becomes knowledge when taken as a totality, i.e., through all its mediations, not through its individual intentions."[14] In the case of Thomas Bernhard, to survey the totality through all its mediations means above all grasping the significance of his style and tone, which are *ironic*. The aggressive, mannered literary technique—long and striking passages of artful rant, inflated complaints, pseudo-philosophical pessimism—conveys the sense of a poetic persona that is grotesquely, satirically exaggerated.

Disguised as philosophy, literary irony defines Strauch and the meaning of his cantankerous disposition. The buffoonery of Strauch's all-consuming hatred establishes him as an ironic figure. His outlandish carping implies a standpoint from which to comprehend the novel as a whole. Strauch may have grasped the true horror of life, as he claims, but the novel *Frost* reveals the pessimistic comedy of his outlook. The irony, achieved through caricature, distortion, the magnification of Strauch and his complaints to the point of parody, sets his viewpoint in perspective. In addition, his young friend is finally not taken in by his misanthropy. Irony undercuts Strauch by overstating his bitterness, by insinuating a saner perspective, by revealing him to be alienated beyond recall. In this, Bernhard is not unlike Kafka.

Writing on Kafka, Walker Percy has described what he calls the aesthetic reversal of alienation.[15] It applies as well to Bernhard's fiction. Percy argues that the modern literature of alienation, and Kafka in particular, surmounts the problem by pointing at it and giving it a name. The literature of alienation cannot offer a pathway to redemption, and it does not claim to; but it recognizes and criticizes the modern condition for what it is. Such literature does not aim to transform the human condition, but merely to understand it.

Bernhard's personal experience is relevant here. He discovered the power of literary naming when he was a teen-ager slowly convalescing at Grafenhof, the welfare sanatorium for tuberculosis patients at which he was interned. Alienated from his peers, his mother dying of cancer in a different hospital, himself dangerously ill, and bored nearly to death, Bernhard turned to writing ("I existed only through my writing") and to music ("my only true passion") as a connection to life. Writing and music were part of Bernhard's revolt against Grafenhof, its doctors, "the inevitability of its laws." Reading, too, played its part: Trakl, Verlaine, Dostoyevsky. "The monstrous quality of *The Demons* made me strong," he wrote of Dostoyevsky.

When Bernhard finally left Grafenhof, he went in pursuit of the demons that tormented him. Literature was the vehicle of his pursuit. His demons, I think, are abundant in the landscape of *Frost*. Its plot, though minimal, revolves around the conversations between a "pilgrim" figure (a latter-day

Gulliver among the Yahoos of Austria) and Strauch, his demonic "mentor." Because Bernhard has all but dispensed with the convention of plot, the tale's setting takes on an enlarged significance. Weng is a small and backward community set in the wilderness of a remote mountain region. Bernhard accentuates the symbolically rich idea of Austrian *wilderness* in many of his works: as setting it gives an outward form to inward bewilderment. Rugged mountains, desolate forests, wild beasts, dangerous rivers, and the like express Bernhard's vision of human nature. So it is that the people of Weng (again, much like Swift's Yahoos) embody the animal instincts and appetites of the wilderness within.

The young spy takes up residence in a local inn where he witnesses the daily exchanges between Strauch and the other denizens of Weng. The inn is the scene of brutish eating and drinking; the slatternly landlady indulges her sexual appetite freely; her paramour, the so-called *Wasenmeister,* trafficks in the carcasses of dead animals. Casual violence and murders are commonplace in Weng. The local populace is rife with venereal disease, tuberculosis, and rickets. Incest spawns the deformity and feeblemindedness that give Weng its fundamental character. Bernhard's imaginary village offers a vivid fictional realization of human bewilderment as a moral wilderness. Its demons are disease, raw instinct, and moral depravity; and they issue directly from nature, or at least seem to.

I shall argue later that Bernhardian nature must be understood as a metaphorical transposition of history. But before turning to that question, the basic anti-Rousseauist myth of nature in the fiction must be addressed. "I hate nature," says Bernhard in his autobiographical novel *Wittgensteins Neffe* (1982; translated as *Wittgenstein's Nephew,* 1989), "because it is killing me."

> I live in the country only because the doctors have told me that I must live *in the country* if I want to survive—for no other reason. In fact I love everything except nature, because it is killing me; I have become familiar with the malignity and implacability of nature through the way it has dealt with my own body and soul, and being unable to contemplate the beauties of nature without at the same time contemplating its malignity and implacability, I fear it and avoid it whenever I can.

Disease is nature's primary representative. Bernhard's preoccupation with disease has more in common with Dostoyevsky and even Thomas Mann than with the romantic poet Novalis, the mystic poet of the romantic era to whom he occasionally alludes. As in Mann and Dostoyevsky, disease generates a sense of critical detachment from average life. It makes Bernhard's protagonists rebellious against the status quo and forces them to take refuge in cerebration. And, as Bernhard tries to show in his meditations on his own struggle against disease, it serves the positive function of keeping the writer in touch with basal humanity. The clarity that Bernhard vaunts derives from his contact with such elemental experience. Presumably his distaste for prestigious clubs and literary societies also stems from his insistence on remaining in touch with what is most basic. To succumb to the accolades of his peers would mean a betrayal of his art's basic principle.

In Bernhard's fiction disease is not a mystical quantity. Rather, it symbolizes the claims of death on life. Disease makes death visible, as it were, to the perceptive mind. In addition, corruption of the body not only mirrors a corrupt soul but *is* one, because in Bernhard's world the spirit is a prisoner of the body. In one of the key scenes of *Frost,* Strauch stumbles across the mangled remains of some freshly slaughtered cattle. Poachers have hastily butchered them and then wastefully abandoned the carcasses in a lonely stretch of forest. Strauch's confrontation with the scattered entrails and severed heads expresses outwardly the inner confrontation with death that tortures him. The grisly scene is a tableau of his own inescapable, animal fate. "The only wisdom is slaughterhouse wisdom," wails Strauch in a visceral outburst of rancor against his nature. His outcry is a protest against the soul's captivity in the flesh.

The callow narrator's encounter with Strauch is likewise an encounter with the suppressed inner realm. Bernhard forces his inexperienced pilgrim and, with him, the reader to look at and contemplate a realm in which minds and bodies are twisted almost beyond recognition. Impulses and fears that sleep beneath layers of civilized convention are wakened in a spirit that recalls the paintings of Breughel and Bosch, or the "Theater of Cruelty" of Antonin Artaud, Bernhard's old favorite, or the paintings of Francis Bacon. The inwardness that Bernhard makes visible has little to do with that addressed by the psychological novel. Rather than explore feelings and motives, Bernhard attempts to capture in fictional form the latent spirit of the modern condition, as much collective as personal. Bernhard's protagonists dwell on death because death has been systematically purged from modern consciousness. His protagonists suffer from the opposite fate: they cannot forget death for a moment. The nervous sleeplessness that afflicts Strauch and other Bernhard protagonists sums up their paralyzing inability to forget.

The task of the reader, like that of the narrator, is to come to some kind of understanding of Strauch and his obsessions. To do so does not entail either accepting or rejecting Strauch's theories about life. It means developing a sense of his struggle, for the meaning of Bernhard's writing lies nowhere but in the verbal struggle against death. Strauch actively seeks out the worst in order to embody it, then live on out of sheer contempt for it. But he is no model for the young protagonist. By the end of the book the narrator manages to break the deadly spell that binds him to Strauch. He leaves Weng after twenty-six days, the vicarious burden of Strauch's misery having become unendurable. His action disproves Strauch's dictum that "no one ever knows the decisive moment," an obscure maxim that Bernhard's various protagonists espouse with fanatic certainty. When the narrator returns to his life in the lowlands, when he has weathered his foray into the heart of darkness, he reads a newspaper report from Weng. A man there, Strauch, is missing and presumed dead. It was Strauch who had been unable to recognize the decisive moment.

Book reviewers in Austria, West Germany, and Switzerland did not greet *Frost* with universal enthusiasm. But the reception, both positive and negative, established Bernhard as a literary presence.[16] During the next few years Bernhard continued to experiment with the prose style and basic motifs that he had begun to develop in *Frost*. In two slighter works, *Amras* (1964) and *Ungenach* (1968)—and in one novel, *Verstörung* (1967; translated as *Gargoyles*, 1970)— Bernhard's characteristic imagery, language, and configuration of characters begin to take on recognizable contours. *Frost* had contained most of the basic features; the Austrian microcosm, the hostility of nature, the failed or would-be genius, the family that fails to understand its gifted son, the sister-brother problem. But in *Frost* these issues are mostly marginal. We know, for instance, that Strauch lived with his sister in Weng during the war, but it remains an unintelligible detail until the motif is developed in later works. Only then do such themes begin to fall into a pattern.

In *Frost* the inn is the focal point of social interaction and a symbol of Austrian life. In later works the burden of attention shifts toward a more private setting. As in Freud, the family comes to represent civilization's germinal cell, and, more specifically, it stands as a microcosm for Bernhard's view of Austrian civilization in particular. He seldom strays from a basic pattern of images involving family and nation. The lineage in question is usually that of the landed gentry encrusted with the prestige of Old

Austria. The family's ancient estate—tower, castle, or villa—makes for an imposing and concrete symbol of the tradition in decay. The estate itself will be in disrepair or even in ruins, as a visible sign of Austria's declining spiritual estate.

The last son of the clan, a childless bachelor, is an eccentric intellectual who refuses to comply with the family's wish that he carry on its tradition. His only wish is to annihilate the last vestige of all that his family stood for. In *Ungenach,* for example, the gifted son is Robert Zoiss. He has fled the family and Ungenach (the family landholding) to take up a post in mathematics at Stanford University. When the rest of the detested Zoiss clan has at last died out, ownership of Ungenach falls to him, its last living member. He decides to liquidate Ungenach and give away everything that has to do with it. He is, as the family lawyer points out, a destroyer of history, actively trying to expunge his own and his family's past. The specter of Nazism is a strong but unspoken presence in the family history. Its bloodline is that of Austria itself.

The situation in *Amras* is similar. Bernhard imagines an entire family that has tried to commit suicide as a group—symbolic of Austria's self-destructive participation in Hitler's Reich. Unexpectedly, two sons survive and withdraw into a lonely tower at Amras, near Innsbruck. The decrepit tower is all that remains of the family's once vast holdings. In Bernhard's modest inventory of images the tower or any of its ramified forms (castle, estate, or mansion) embodies the fate of Old Austria: faded glory, decay, collapse.

The fate of the brothers themselves is likewise paradigmatic. One, the narrator, is a scientific researcher, and the other, a gifted musician, is sickly and suffers from epilepsy. The disease, supposedly transmitted from generation to generation in the unwholesome region of their birth, is Bernhard's metaphor for Austrian identity. To be born an Austrian means to be the victim of a congenital defect from which no recovery is possible: history is heredity. The musical brother, his sensitive artist's soul reflected in his frail constitution, soon dies by his own hand. Bernhard leads us to surmise that the artist cannot survive in the poisonous atmosphere of Austria. The stronger brother, the scientist, lives on, but without joy or hope. He exists mechanically among ignorant woodcutters with whom he cannot communicate.

The figurative point of the brothers' fate is one that Bernhard reiterated vehemently in books, interviews, and speeches throughout his career. To be artistically or intellectually gifted in Austria amounts to exile or death. "Genius and Austria don't mix," says Reger, one of Bernhard's opinionated curmudgeons; "in Austria you have to be a mediocrity in order to have a say and be taken seriously, a man of plodding mind and provincial fakery, a man whose head is absolutely suited to a minuscule nation." Although Bernhard does not bother to support such claims with examples, many cases come to mind: Mozart, Mahler, Freud, Trakl, Wittgenstein, Schönberg, Broch, Musil, and Kurt Gödel to say nothing of Austria's massacred Jewry. The trauma of such losses pervades all of Bernhard's fiction and drama. Austria itself is an open wound, as he once put it, that can no longer be healed.

The posthistorical melancholy of *Frost* had explicitly historical roots. Strauch cites the depredations of World War II as the reason for spiritual abasement of Weng. But in works after *Frost*, Bernhard seldom feels obliged to offer any kind of rational explanation for the human degradation and for Austrian decline. Only occasionally does he make remarks that help to clarify the historical presuppositions of his writing. In 1966, for example, responding to a poll about Austrian art and politics, Bernhard asserted that the twentieth century's "global proletarian revolt" set Austria on a course of irreversible cultural and political decline: "Today, half a century after the destruction of the empire, its patrimony is exhausted, its heirs are bankrupt."[17] The language of inheritance and heredity is characteristic, linking history with ontology. Even more telling is the central metaphor in *Amras* of a hereditary disease that debilitates an entire region.

Disease is Bernhard's chief metaphor for Austria's degeneration. The mind succumbs to madness; the body, the family, and the nation fall prey to disease and death. Bernhard assimilates history to a private metaphysics expressed in metaphors of disease and death. His apocalyptic imagery stems from his intuitive ethics, from his personal outrage against Austria, its history and his own fate there. The final origin of apocalypse is nature itself, which for Bernhard is also an ethically conditioned metaphor. The moral corruption of modernity is mirrored in the decay of the body, whether it be the body of the individual or the body politic. The idea of bodily pollution and decay as natural process fascinates him, though he makes no allowance for the traditionally mythic notion of a cycle in which renewal follows degeneration. Consequently, Bernhard banishes erotic pleasure from his imaginary Austria. Because it is conventionally associated with procreation, renewal, transcendence, and utopia, the pleasure of human sexuality cannot figure into Bernhard's universe. When sex finds a place in his work at all, it is a vile act, often an incestuous one but more frequently simply the crime of setting children into a despicable world.

"Children," says Prince Saurau of *Gargoyles,* "are probably conceived and dragged into the world by their parents out of nothing but *schadenfreude* and the greatest imaginable lack of consideration."

Gargoyles

In *Verstörung* (Derangement, 1967), which appeared in English under the title *Gargoyles* (1970), Bernhard fastens his gaze on the horrors that nature can inflict on mind and body. As in *Frost,* the premise of the novel's limited action is the pilgrimage of a novice. This time a young mining student accompanies his father, who is a country doctor, on a series of house calls. The setting is once again the inhospitable backcountry of mountainous Styria. In visit after visit the student of mining becomes a miner of human souls as his insight into human depravity deepens. For the first time in his life he must contemplate the meaning of wife-beating, incest, pederasty, madness, and cruelties of every perverted sort. Nature, expressed here as a deceptively beautiful setting that promotes disease and mental illness, seems to mock the pretensions of human dignity. Human nature, deceitful and base, is merely an extension of nature itself.

It might be useful to regard the tormented souls of *Gargoyles*—the inexact though felicitous English title for *Verstörung*—as modern descendants of the deformed, degraded creatures in the paintings of Hieronymus Bosch. Bernhard's fictional Austria, like Bosch's "Garden of Earthly Delights," is a comic teratology of human vice and agony. Both artists depict landscapes beset with every extravagant transgression and hidden fear. Neither offers the least hint of hope or redemption from hellish suffering. Bernhard shares with Bosch a deep pessimism about man's innermost nature, one that finds its expression in allegory.

Unlike the more conventional psychological realism commonly associated with the novel, allegorical representation explores a wider, more abstractly conceived inwardness. Consequently Bernhard's figures lack psychological depth. They exist more as personified ideas than as plausibly imagined people. "In my books," writes Bernhard with his own italics, "everything is *artificial,* that is, all figures, events, incidents, take place on a stage and this *theatrical space* is completely dark."[18] The detached, staged quality suggests that Bernhard would like to concentrate our detached attention on the shared fears, conflicts, and unpleasant impulses that most of us manage to repress most of the time. Artificiality gives them sharpened contours, makes them accessible to detached consideration.

To put it more simply, Bernhard asks what it would be like if the mind were not able to forget the omnipresence of death. Among other things, the mind's unblinking vigilance would make it difficult to sleep, an affliction common among Bernhard's figures. Strauch is plagued by sleepless nights, as is the principal madman in *Gargoyles,* Prince Saurau, who suffers from an even more pronounced inability to sleep. Prince Saurau is a deranged insomniac who lives with what remains of his family at Hochgobernitz, the ancestral family castle. As soon as the doctor and his son arrive, Saurau launches into a monologue that takes up over half of the novel. The prince is a man in whom the narrative impulse is supreme. He rambles with hypnotic lucidity from topic to topic, transforming his entire world into verbal rubble. He roams the backwashes of mind and memory in pursuit of a settled reality, or at least some kind of order to things. A brief excerpt can only hint at the irrational power of the whole:

> Then he said: "My sisters but also my daughters always try to keep me going by fraudulent means, deceptions major and minor, but especially through one scandalous ruse: *their attention.* Each basically knows," he said, "that the world will collapse if I am suddenly not here anymore. If I lose interest and have myself laid out in the summer cottage. I plan to have myself laid out in the summer cottage like my father. A dead father," he said, "really instills fear. Often I think for hours on end of nothing but the mailman. The mail has got to come, I think. Mail! Mail! Mail! *News!*"

Communication, family, and death are Saurau's main interests, bound up as they are with the fate of Hochgobernitz. He is the patriarch of a moribund clan whose life and history center on the castle. It, like Saurau and his family, is a pathetic relic of Old Austria. Saurau lives in fear of his expatriate son who, like Zoiss in *Ungenach* or Franz-Josef in *Auslöschung* (Obliteration, 1986), will someday return from exile to liquidate the estate after the old prince is dead.

Saurau's ruminations, like those of Strauch in *Frost,* have a comic warp. For example, when the prince relates the events of his own father's last days—a brutal story of insanity and suicide—parts of the tale pass over into grotesque slapstick: "'He ripped the decisive pages out of what had been his favorite books,' said the prince, 'for instance Schopenhauer's *World as Will and Idea,* which he had taken from the library to his room. He ate them,' said the prince." The joke is on philosophy and art, and so also on the novel. Schopenhauer, whose philosophy famously ascribes transcendent qualities to art and aesthetic contemplation, had always been the elder Saurau's favorite "nourishment" (*Nahrung*), but what feeds the mind does not nourish the body. The death of the body obliterates the mind it contains. Art and philosophy, nourishment for the mind, do not deliver the promised transcendence. As an untranscendent work of art Bernhard's novel promises nothing. It merely contemplates the prospect of nothingness.

The act of contemplation has a definite structure in *Frost* and *Gargoyles*, and in many of the later novels. Bernhard likes to divide his fiction between two unequal perspectives. The first is a "witness" figure who narrates his experience of the stronger protagonist. The medical student in *Frost* and the mining student in *Gargoyles* are witnesses to the powerful, if perverse, individualism and intellect of Strauch and Saurau. The witnesses confront vicariously, through their mentors, all that otherwise had been unthinkable in their lives. They witness a world of spiritualized cruelty and inner violence at a remove, via the mad protagonist. For the main protagonist himself there can be no return; he lacks the necessary distance, the ability to forget. But the chastened witness, who is also a proxy for the reader, eventually makes his way back to a more humane reality. In his later fiction Bernhard reverses the perspective, though the basic structure remains intact.

But why does Bernhard give us these observing, reporting figures in *Frost* and *Gargoyles?* They are foils to the monstrous cynicism of Strauch and Saurau. Bernhard experiments with the vision his extremists offer; he makes them articulate, persuasive by the sheer force of their astonishing verbal performances; he enjoys contemplating the arguments that they produce. But they are not philosophically persuasive. Strauch and Saurau are quixotic malcontents, permanently at war with the way the world is. They absolutely refuse to accept it, and this refusal consigns them to ever deepening alienation. What they see is expressed with vigor and clarity, but they see only what is hateful and detestable in human nature. If their vision can be described as an embittered version of quixotry, then the two young observers play the role of a Sancho Panza—a pedestrian reality principle. They are strongly affected by the convictions of the quixotic master, but they do not finally succumb to his mad vision.

NOTES

1. Curiously, in his cheerful book on Austrian national consciousness from 1938 to 1978, Felix Kreissler stresses only the expatriate generation of modernism and ignores the importance of cultural activity that took place on postwar Austrian soil: *Der Österreicher und seine Nation* (Vienna: Böhlau, 1984) 316–71.

2. "The Austrians, being congenital opportunists, are cringers," says Bernhard's uncharitable protagonist of *Old Masters,* "and they live by cover-ups and forgetting." The election of Kurt Waldheim to the post of president in 1986 caused an international uproar when it was discovered that for many years he had concealed his activities as a lieutenant in Hitler's Wehrmacht during World War II. The upshot of the controversy has been a closer international scrutiny of Austria's political history and identity. For a judicious account see Melanie A. Sully, "The Waldheim Connection," *Conquering the Past: Austrian Nazism Yesterday and Today,* edited by F. Parkinson (Detroit: Wayne State University Press, 1989) 294–312.

3. Unlike famous composers and expensive ski resorts, the culturally conservative writers of postwar Austria remain little known outside of German-speaking countries. The names Franz Csokor, Herbert Eisenreich, and Fritz Hochwälder are not likely to sound familiar to anyone except Austrians. Even Heimito von Doderer, the great mid-century novelist of Austrian history and manners, has found only a small international following. Yet within Austria these literary conservatives remain a strong presence. Wendelin Schmidt-Dengler, "Die unheiligen Experimente: Zur Anpassung der Konvention in der Moderne," *Literatur der Nachkriegszeit in der fünfziger Jahre in Österreich,* ed. Friedrich Aspetsberger et al. (Vienna: Österreichische Verlagsanstalt," 1984; "Österreichische Progressivliteratur nach 1945," *Protokolle* 10 (1975): 337–50; on subventions see Georg Schmid, "'Die falschen Fuffziger': Kulturpolitische Tendenzen der fünfziger Jahre in Österreich," Aspetsberger 7–23; Joseph McVeigh, "Politics and Literature in Austria after 1945," *German Quarterly* 61 (1988): 1–21. Cf. Harald Jardos and Manfred Wagner, *Some Aspects of Cultural Policy in Austria* (UNESCO, 1981), 26f, 51ff; and Franz Hofecker, "State Subsidies in Austria," *Austria Today,* No. 4 (1988): 43–45.

4. Rüdiger Wischenbart, "Zur Auseinandersetzung mit der Moderne," Aspetsberger 351–56.

5. "Politische Morgenandacht," *Wort in der Zeit* 12 (1966): 11–13.

6. Bernhard even more pointedly asserts his skeptical attitude toward language in his Büchner Prize acceptance speech, "Nie und mit nichts fertig werden," in *Deutsche Akademie für Sprache und Dichtung, Jahrbuch 1970* (Heidelberg and Darmstadt: Schneider, 1971), 83–84.

7. Kurt Hofmann, *Aus Gesprächen mit Thomas Bernhard* (Vienna: Löcker, 1989) 48. In 1989 Bernhard published a short novel that he wrote during the 50s. *In der Höhe: Rettungsversuch, Unsinn* (Up High: Attempt at Rescue, Nonsense) consists of verbal tatters of thought and experience without much connective narrative. His more or less surrealist approach to writing at the time was abandoned in his later novels.

8. A bibliography of Bernhard's newspaper pieces has been assembled by Christian Klug: "Thomas Bernhard's Arbeiten für *Das Demokratische Volksblatt* 1952–1954," *Modern Austrian Literature* 21, Nos. 3/4 (1988): 165–166.

9. Hofmann, 27.

10. "4 Stunden stramm gestanden," *Neues Forum* 19 (May 1972): 47.

11. *die rosen der einöde: fünf sätze für ballett, stimmen, und orchester* (Frankfurt am Main: Fischer, 1959).

12. The three dramas and *Köpfe,* the musical work, remain unpublished. They were staged on 22 July 1960 at Maria-Saal in Carinthia. Jens Dittmar, ed. *Thomas Bernhard Werkgeschichte* (Frankfurt am Main: Suhrkamp, 1981) 39–45.

13. "Ein Sinnbild der großen Kälte," *Die Zeit,* 21 June 1963. For many years Zuckmayer lived in Henndorf, the village near Salzburg in which Bernhard grew up. Johannes Freumbichler enjoyed some support from Zuckmayer, and consequently Bernhard knew the famous writer personally. Ingeborg Bachmann has emphasized the influence of Zuckmayer on Bernhard in her essay "Thomas Bernhard: Ein Versuch," *Werke* 4 (Munich and Zurich: Piper, 1978) 361–64.

14. Theodor Adorno, "Reconcilation under Duress," *Aesthetics and Politics,* Ernst Bloch et al (London: Verso, 1986) 168.

15. Walker Percy, "The Man on the Train," *The Message in the Bottle* (New York: Farrar Straus and Giroux, 1987) 83–100.

16. See Anneliese Botond's collection of early praise in *Über Thomas Bernhard* (Frankfurt am Main: Suhrkamp, 1970); for a characteristically hostile response to Bernard see Herbert Eisenreich's "Irrsinn im Alpenland," *Der Spiegel,* 1 May 1967: 164–67.

17. "Politische Morgenandacht," 11–13.

18. "Drei Tage," *Der Italiener* (Salzburg: Residenz, 1971) 150.

CHAPTER THREE

Sacrificial Sisters: *The Lime Works* and *Correction*

The Lime Works appeared in West Germany in 1970. The casual reader of this novel in the 1990s may easily forget that it appeared against the backdrop of considerable political fervor in the literary world, especially in the Federal Republic of Germany, where Bernhard's books found their largest audience. The poet and activist Hans Magnus Enzensberger, a good index to the spirit of the 60s, declared in an influential essay of 1968 that literature, in its politically noncommital forms, was dead.[1] He enjoined the moribund representatives of mere fiction to make way for the historically and politically informed literature of "factography" that draws on courtroom protocols, historical documents, and eyewitness accounts for its content. He had in mind documentary modes, such as his *Verhör von Habana* (1970; *The Havana Inquiry,* 1974), which deals with prisoners from the Bay of Pigs incident. Better known are Peter Weiss's *Die Ermittlung* (1965; *The Investigation,* 1966), which draws on source material from the trial of Auschwitz guards and administrators; or Rolf Hochhuth's *Der Stellvertreter* (1963; *The Deputy,* 1963), which attempts to document the passive complicity of the Catholic Church in Nazi crimes; or Heinar Kipphardt's *In der Sache J. Robert Oppenheimer* (1964; *In the Matter of J. Robert Oppenheimer,* 1968), which purports to be a factual account of the American physicist's moral and legal dilemmas.

In sharp opposition to such aims Thomas Bernhard wrote plays and novels that systematically dismantle the pretense of truth in literature. *The Lime Works* is a prime example. It throws into doubt the possibility of knowing facts with authoritative certainty, whether they be political, historical, social, or personal. Bernhard's novel rejects the literature of fact and commitment in at least two ways: first, by proceeding in accordance with a highly indirect narrative technique that mocks the authenticity of reportage as an outright impossibility; second, by telling a tale of withdrawal, resignation, and defeat. The protagonist's insane commitment to truth and perfection only leads him to destruction.

SACRIFICIAL SISTERS

Let us turn first to Bernhard's approach to writing. The basic tool of representation, language, inevitably distorts whatever it takes as its object. In his memoirs Bernhard argues that "description makes something clear which accords with the describer's *aspiration* to truth but not with truth itself, for truth is quite impossible to communicate."[2] Bernhard builds the idea into the structure of his book as a discontinuity between the storyteller and his tale: the narrator is never quite sure of his facts. While his "aspiration" to truth is plain, the facts that constitute his true story remain partially hidden.

The Lime Works

The Lime Works, one of Bernhard's best and most oppressive stories, recounts the "facts," trivial and significant alike, that lead up to the shooting death of an invalid woman in a squalid Austrian backwater town. The narrative focuses on the killer, a man named Konrad. He is an eccentric autodidact in his fifties who has withdrawn with his handicapped wife to the book's eponymous lime works in order to work undisturbed on a scientific book. But after many years of agonized research his project has come to nothing. On Christmas Eve he shot and killed his wife, a woman permanently confined to a wheelchair. The narrator—an insurance salesman whose name we never learn—proceeds to tell all he has heard about the Konrads in local inns and taverns. He weaves his report from the threads of supposition, hearsay, and gossip. No authoritative perspective governs the tale:

> And I have believed in this figment of your imagination for twenty years! she is supposed to have shouted several times on the evening before the bloody deed (as they put it at Laska's), possibly, says Fro, that made him, Konrad, shoot his wife. On the other hand, he, Konrad, is supposed to have been tender toward his wife again for the first time in ages exactly on the evening before he shot her (so they say at the Lanner). Word has it in the Gmachl that Konrad *took his own sweet time* in planning the bloody deed, in the Stiegler they are still talking today about a *sudden impulse,* no matter whether, as they also say at Lanner's, it was *cold-blooded premeditated murder,* or, as at the Gmachl, *an insane act,* at Laska's they also suspect that Konrad did not want to shoot his wife at all, that he was trying to clean his Mannlicher carbine for the first time after a long while. . . . To this day Konrad, supposedly, has not furthered matters with even the least comment about the deed, he

purportedly just sits in jail at Wels, an utterly broken man, without answering any of the hundreds and probably thousands of questions being put to him.

Why all the to-and-fro among competing and only partially informed points of view? Obviously the narrative voice does not claim to establish and verify the accuracy of his story. Curiosity and the impulse to gossip dominate the narrator's wish to tell what he "knows." We must assume that Bernhard's gnarl of clichés and indirections suggests the very impossibility of saying, with certainty, exactly what the truth is. Or as Konrad puts it, words debase and destroy the thought they are supposed to express. Thus he must continually correct and rewrite his manuscript, much like the protagonist of the later novel, *Correction*. The perfection they seek, truth, is unattainable because language cannot support the burden of perfection.

Language and storytelling never travel straight to the mark. They arrive, if at all, by way of circumlocution and innuendo, symbol and allegory. So it is with the governing metaphor of the novel, the lime works that Konrad inhabits with his wife. It expresses as mute image the ambiguity of knowing. Significantly, we never learn exactly what the abandoned quarry looks like, and we are never told how the Konrads' house is situated with regard to it. We only know that they live at the derelict lime works, an old stonework labyrinth long in the possession of Konrad's family. The truth of matters such as Konrad's innermost need to kill his wife is as labyrinthine and silent as the lime works into which Konrad has withdrawn.

All our knowledge about the lime works and Konrad's doings there comes to us via our "reporter," an insurance agent. No doubt Bernhard is alluding here to Franz Kafka, German literature's most renowned insurance official. Kafka's fiction provides the premier example of a circuitous, never-ending web of opinions and facts that finally add up to nothing. Moreover, Kafka's narrators always adhere rigorously to the same narratological precept that structures *The Lime Works:* only one point of view, the perspective of a single consciousness, is permitted to speak; all else is rumor, conjecture, and reportage. The novel's carefully framed point of view imposes significant limits on Bernhard's inquiry into the nature of his protagonist.

Like most of Bernhard's fiction, *The Lime Works* paradoxically seeks to sound out the unfathomable depths of the self. Yet the admission that his task is impossible does not deter him. Bits and pieces of insight offer themselves to the inquiring mind, even if ultimate success will always elude it.

To make matters even more complicated, Bernhard refuses to proceed by the rules of the traditional psychological novel, to say nothing of the categories of psychoanalysis. His literary exploration of the inner life proceeds by other means. It will be useful to digress for a moment in order to compare Bernhard's Konrad to the killer Moosbrugger in Robert Musil's unfinished masterpiece of the 1930s, *The Man without Qualities*. The killer in Musil's novel presents a scientific and legal enigma to the law courts and psychologists of "Kakania" (Musil's scatological name for Austria). The lawyers and doctors can find no psychological precedents or applicable statutes according to which they can treat his case medically and prosecute it legally. With no guidelines to point the way, Moosbrugger's puzzling existence remains an open sore on the casebooks of Kakania.

Similarly, Konrad's predicament remains outside of finality for the interpreter of Bernhard's novel. His technique of indirection leaves us without a way of clarifying ambiguities. The narrator of a psychological novel would give us access to Konrad's thoughts and feelings; Bernhard's narrator emphasizes that he knows only what the innkeepers and their cronies have reported. The application of psychoanalytic techniques of interpretation would fail to produce results other than what was already implicit in the method itself. So if we are to gain insight into the enigma of Konrad's soul, it must come through the external evidence that Bernhard offers.

The question that must be asked of this book, then, is not "What inner necessity motivates Konrad?" Bernhard operates under the assumption that we cannot fathom the true interior of a human being. This assumption has consequences for his place in the tradition of the novel. By way of comparison with the classics—Flaubert and Stendhal, for example, or Joyce and Proust—it becomes clear that Bernhard's attitude toward the idea of inner life is different. He has more in common with Kafka, who denied the possibility of psychological introspection: "The inner world cannot be observed in the same way that we observe the outer world. At least descriptive psychology is probably on the whole an anthropomorphism, a gnawing at the edges. The inner world can only be lived, not described."[3] Proust and Joyce, Faulkner and Virginia Woolf, are Kafka's opposites. They proceed by offering a view of "the contents of consciousness," to borrow Auerbach's famous phrase. For Kafka, and for Thomas Bernhard, the contents of consciousness are always out of reach. The self is unique and so cannot be described in conventional language. It is a hidden process, ephemeral and unfathomable as a whole. Consequently, Kafka and Bernhard restrict themselves to describing the effects of the inner life on the outward, visible world.

In *The Lime Works* we learn nothing of Konrad's inner life. Instead we must approximate it according to its outward signs. Konrad is an irascible man, utterly withdrawn into his egotistical ambition to write the definitive study of hearing. Over many years he tortures his frail wife with his outlandish project, using her as a guinea pig, dominating her, ignoring her needs and wishes. Ironically, this student of listening seems constitutionally incapable of really listening to his own wife. He turns a deaf ear to her need for family and friends. Against her wishes he has forced her to join him in the lime works. In his flight from the society and culture of his fellow human beings, Konrad has ensconced himself, and her too, in an empty world. At one time they had been great travelers, participants in life. But now Konrad has turned inward. The lime works—his home—expresses the inward turn as visible fact.

From this perspective *The Lime Works* can be seen to be a tale of hypertrophied intellect. Contemptuous of a humane existence among people and things, the intellectual fanatic has reduced himself to any empty ruin of a human being. On his journey inward Konrad inhabits his decaying ruin of a house. What attracts Konrad to the lime works is not a sense of home or rootedness that it offers. Its loneliness appeals to him. His wife would like nothing better than to return to the friends and family of her beloved home at Toblach, but Konrad's selfish obsession causes him to immure himself and her with him in a hollow world. The house does not do the work of an ancestral home, though it had originally belonged to Konrad's family. It holds no memories, no family, not even any furniture, because he has sold it all off in order to finance his fruitless study of hearing. What Konrad thought would be his utopia turns out to be true in too literal a sense. It is a non-place: a derelict building and an abandoned mine in the middle of nowhere.

The lime works is above all a metaphor of the self. On this count it will be instructive to digress briefly in order to compare Bernhard with Musil once again. Ulrich, the protagonist of *The Man without Qualities,* undertakes a similar retreat into the inner life. He has nothing but contempt for the customs, institutions, and other outward things that shape inward life and experience. His self-exploration leads him to discover what he calls "the other condition," a state of inward authenticity that, according to Musil, is mystical in origin. But the turn to mysticism, as Musil well knew, is fraught with moral danger. To turn to the other world entails neglect of this one. Musil did not finish his enormous novel, so we do not know how, or even if, he would have reconciled the need for inward authenticity with the vicissitudes of outward life.

But before examining Bernhard's solution to a similar conflict, we should note one last, but striking, similarity between Musil and Bernhard. Ulrich has a partner in his experimentation with "the other condition." The partner is his sister Agatha. Together they express their contempt for convention—which is identical with their ambition to explore the undiscovered reaches of the inner life—by flirting with the ultimate transgression: incest. But the crime remains only an idea that Ulrich and Agatha do not finally realize. Bernhard carries out the imaginary experiment more ruthlessly than Musil did. Konrad's wife is also his half-sister.

In addition, as in *The Man without Qualities,* Bernhard's husband/wife–brother/sister configuration represents a principle of complementarity. Like Ulrich, Konrad is a man of icy intellectuality and unemotional detachment; like Agatha, Konrad's half-sister is a woman of humane feeling who completes, as it were, the deficient man. The more Konrad concentrates on his scientific project, or at least what he imagines to be his life's work, the more his real life withers. The degeneration of his wife's health corresponds inversely with his ever increasing self-absorption. The more deeply he withdraws into his intellectual self, the more helpless her bodily life becomes. The more deeply he becomes mired in the study of hearing, the less he listens to his wife. Only together do Konrad and his wife add up to a whole human being, a unity of intellect and soul. "At bottom," opines one of the gossiping innkeepers, "in killing his wife, Konrad did not primarily kill his wife but, suddenly and without thought, killed himself." The story of the murder is the story of Konrad's self-destruction.

The difference between Musil and Bernhard is revealing. As if in answer to Robert Musil, Bernhard offers a contradictory view of the human soul. For Musil the inner self is the locus of truth and authenticity. For Bernhard the inner self is a void. The inner world turns out to be a utopian construct, a place where there is nothing. At best it is a life-sustaining illusion; at worst—in the hostile formulation of Konrad's wife—a *delusion*.

The wife-sister motif figures prominently in Bernhard's writing. The short narrative *Amras* (1964) features incestuous siblings, as do *An der Baumgrenze* (1969) and *Am Ortler* (1971) and *Vor dem Ruhestand* (1979; *Eve of Retirement, 1982*). The latent significance of sibling incest in Bernhard's writing is no doubt many-sided. But at least three interpretive possibilities stand out. First, incest in Bernhard's Austria suggests a degenerate culture. Postwar Austria, in Bernhard's vision, is a place of insanity, congenital defects, and instincts gone out of control; it is a place rife with the maladies and vices traditionally associated with inbreeding. Bernhardian Austria has turned inward upon itself, become obsessed with its lost greatness, and refused to enter the future. Second, the incest metaphor touches Austria's debauched union with Germany in 1938. This interpretation may sound far-fetched at first, but the motif of specifically *sibling* incest is so persistent, and Bernhard's preoccupation with the decline of German culture (in both Austria and Germany) so intense, that the possibility cannot be ruled out.

Third, and most striking, incest is the only prominent form of sexual desire in Bernhard's fiction. In Musil's fiction incest was the sign of radical individualism, of personalities so strong that no cultural taboo can contain them. Bernhard's use of the incest theme has an element of individualism, but the stress falls heavily on degradation, and especially on the degradation of women. The apparent misogyny of Bernhard's male protagonists must be mediated by a larger understanding of the way his fiction presents sexuality. The protagonists resent, hate, and even fear women because the feminine stands for everything that impinges upon the fanatical pride of male spiritual autonomy: family, commitment, erotic instinct, nourishment of the body. Ultimately, nature itself seems to hold men back from the higher life. When their ambitious intellectual and spiritual projects fail, their self-hatred turns toward the outward representatives of inward failure: women.

The oppression of women in Bernhard's fiction, rightly understood, explores the self-destructive nature of masculine pride. When viewed from the larger perspective, Bernhard's seeming misogyny turns out to be a critique of masculine self-hatred. In Bernhard's writing the attempt to destroy women always discloses the insane and self-destructive impulse of his heroes. They seek to expunge all that is feminine from within themselves. Incest serves to imply that the feminine element is really a part of the man and not some separate realm. Strauch in *Frost* was reduced to his miserable state by the loss of his sister in World War II. In *Amras* the narrator declines into alienated depression after the death of his weaker, more feminine younger brother (for whom he had a strong sexual feeling). *The Lime Works* tells the story of Konrad's slow progress toward annihilation represented as the oppression and murder of his helpless wife. That she is also his sister underscores her meaning as the symbol for his suppressed feminine soul.

She is literally his better half. And in *Correction* the protagonist's pride brings about the death of his beloved sister.

Correction

In 1975 Bernhard published *Korrektur* (translated as *Correction*, 1979). The story focuses on Roithamer, an eccentric genetic scientist who has committed suicide. Much has been made of Roithamer's loose resemblance to Ludwig Wittgenstein, but the comparison has produced no findings that advance our understanding of the book.[4] More revealing are Roithamer's similarities to Konrad, the protagonist of *The Lime Works*. First of all, Konrad and Roithamer are similar in their eccentricities. Like Konrad, Roithamer is an insomniac fanatically devoted to producing a single masterwork. He has become obsessed with designing and building a giant cone-shaped home for his sister to live in. The image of "the Cone," as it is called, belongs to Bernhard's inventory of symbolic towers, castles, lime works, and other imposing and solitary edifices.

These buildings have an identifiable meaning. "Thought," says Prince Saurau in *Gargoyles*, "is always represented as a building inhabitable for longer or shorter periods of time." Bernhard renders the idea literally. In *Gargoyles* the prince inhabits a monstrous world of his own insane devising precisely as he inhabits his castle. Konrad retreats into the lime works as he retreats into his solipsistic thought world. And when Roithamer designs and constructs a monstrous, isolated Cone, he gives architectonic form to his own monstrous individuality and isolation.

It is worth pausing for a moment over a passage from *Gargoyles* that reads as if it were a description of both Konrad and Roithamer. The country doctor ponders the fate of one of his bizarre patients:

> At a crisis in their lives some people seek out a dungeon, voluntarily enter it and devote their lives—which they regard as philosophically oriented—to some scholarly task or some imaginative scientific obsession. They always take with them into their dungeon some creature who is attached to them. In most cases they sooner or later destroy this creature who has entered the dungeon with them and then themselves.

In *Gargoyles* the "creature" in question is the patient's insane half-sister. She brings into view the most important link between Konrad and Roithamer.

The sister, with or without incestuous overtones, is one of Bernhard's key figures. She is silent, dominated, and unfree for reasons to be discussed shortly. The brother is her oppressor. Like Konrad before him, Roithamer oppresses and finally destroys his sister. He does not marry her, as Konrad did, but all the same he attempts to possess her in an extraordinary way. Roithamer envisions, designs, and builds his Cone as the perfect home for his sister, an expression of his love for her. In reality it is a lonely dungeon in which he holds her captive and in which she perishes. Though he does not lay a hand on her, his demented love for her destroys her as surely as Konrad compelled his sister to live in the lime works and finally shot her in the head.

In general Bernhard's women do not fare well. They tend either to be victimized by men or they are repulsive harridans. To make matters worse, Bernhard frequently gives his male protagonists misogynistic attitudes. Roithamer is a case in point:

> People are forever denying the proven fact, so Roithamer, the simple fact of nature's workings, that the female sex, because it is female, nobody dares to say it in so many words nowadays, that the female sex is anti-intellectual and emotionally predisposed to champion emotion, that it is in fact against intellect in all its possible aspects just as it is emotionally predisposed to emotion in all its possible aspects, so Roithamer.[5]

It is Bernhard's ruthless style to let outrageous opinions stand without comment or context, without nuance or ironic winks to the reader. As a consequence there have been attempts to discredit him for sundry depravities, including misogyny.[6] Bernhard, who prided himself on being a troublemaker, no doubt enjoyed the spectacle of the fury and scorn he stirred up. But whether or not he was really a woman hater remains unclear. It seems reasonable to assume that the aim of his inflammatory strutting is to provoke, not to edify or to persuade. In any case, the belligerent antifeminism of his protagonists has drawn attention away from the metaphorical role that he allots to his women characters.

The main idea is plainest in *Correction*. Roithamer describes the sister as "a sort of second and superior self." His sister is the part of himself he has always suppressed and rejected. In a configuration reminiscent of *Amras* the sister is artistic, emotional, more fully human than the coldly intellectual brother. While Roithamer may be an opponent of all that is feminine, the novel implies that his gravest flaw is the absence of a soul, which the feminine embodies. In destroying his sister, Roithamer destroys himself. He merely draws the consequences when he commits suicide.

Bernhard lends an added dimension of meaning to the Cone and the death it symbolizes by means of Roithamer's childhood friend, Höller. It is Höller who originally gives Roithamer the idea of constructing a house for his sister. Höller had long since moved his family out of town into an isolated house of his own design, which he built for them high above the dangerous Aurach gorge. But apart from the house idea there is another important feature that links Roithamer's inner life to Höller's: taxidermy. Höller makes his living by stuffing dead animals:

> Roithamer had always spoken at length about Höller's work, his procedures in preserving, stuffing andsoforth all kinds of animals, every possible kind of fowl, Roithamer had always profited, so he himself said, from watching Höller at work, seeing how those dead creatures were dissected and stuffed and sewed up. For Roithamer . . . these products of nature, stuffed and turned into artifacts, always provided an occasion for various reflections on nature and art and art and nature.[7]

Höller's vaguely sinister personality and his life's work, preserving dead animals, resonate eerily with Roithamer's scheme for his sister. He wants to embalm her by forcing her to live in his tomblike Cone.

The Cone is intended for the sister *alone*. So extreme is Roithamer's insistence on this point that he locates his conical mausoleum at the exact center of the vast and unpopulated Kobernausser Forest. There he imprisons his beloved alter ego, repeatedly promising her "supreme happiness," only to discover that she drops dead in it. The cause of her abrupt death is not specified, but as Roithamer gradually comes to see, the ruthless implementation of his idea—without regard for his sister's wishes—has killed her. Like Konrad's lime works, the Cone is an empty, soulless, uninhabitable dungeon. The Cone stands as image of Roithamer's murderously egocentric, hyperintellectual inner self.

The sister's first role, then, is to reflect the protagonist's inward failure. But there accrues to her yet another significance, this one historical. Bernhard's women frequently embody his one-sided version of Austrian history. Roithamer's family is a microcosm of modern Austria. The father belongs to a formerly aristocratic clan that has gone to seed and is now on the verge of dying out. In order to secure heirs he has married a slovenly, vulgar woman because she is, as he puts it, a "good breeder." But she is also ignorant, venal, lazy, and just plain mean. She personifies for Bernhard the fate of modern Austria: the once grand and spiritual empire that has sunk to the lowest level.

The sister is her opposite. She, like Roithamer, is the father's favorite because she takes after his side of the family. She is an artist, a sensitive and reflective soul. But she cannot thrive in an atmosphere dominated by the repulsive mother, the robust daughter of a butcher. The fragile sister suffers from bouts of madness. Worst of all, her brother, who claims to love her, wants to save her from the degenerate family by isolating her in his private world. The setting of Roithamer's grand scheme, as is typical for Bernhard, also has significance. The mad builder has chosen a site at the exact center of the Kobernausser Forest, a desolate wilderness in Upper Austria. As it happens, the tract of land once belonged to a member of the Habsburg clan, but the royal family has been long since dispossessed by the modern state of Austria. The situation encapsulates the Bernhard scenario of historical decline. Austria's former greatness has been usurped by the state—"a totally decrepit, public menace of a state, as Roithamer said again and again"—that has transformed it into a wilderness, like Konrad's lime works, that is empty and abandoned.

The *wilderness* metaphor returns us once more to the imagery of Roithamer's inner self. By insisting on the exact center of the Kobernausser Forest as a building site, the middle of nowhere, Bernhard calls our attention to the true state of his hero's impoverished inner life. He attempts to enrich it by imprisoning his sister there, but he only succeeds in destroying her and then himself. The sister—silent, absent, venerated—personifies the lost Austria. Roithamer intends to preserve her, artificially, in the dreadful solitude of the Kobernausser Forest.

When she dies, Roithamer attempts to grasp what has happened by writing a manuscript that he calls *Altensam and Everything Connected with Altensam, with Special Attention to the Cone* (Altensam is the name of the family estate). His manuscript is the source of the novel. Roithamer writes and rewrites and ceaselessly "corrects" his text in an attempt to reach the truth. Finally, on the way to his sister's funeral, he abruptly realizes "that everything I'd described in my manuscript was not so, that everything is always different from the way it's been described. . . . Everything I'd described was all wrong."[8] We must assume that this includes what he wrote about his sister. He believed that he was giving her the supreme gift in building the Cone for her to live in. He had believed that the Cone would be her supreme happiness. When it killed her, he even persisted in the delusion that she must have died of perfect joy: "Supreme happiness, so Roithamer, as the instant cause of my sister's death, so Roithamer."[9] As the deluded genius proceeds toward his sister's funeral, he gradually realizes that the idea of building a Cone for her "was nothing but a mad aberration, but he'd have to accept responsibility for this mad aberration and take it to its logical conclusion."

> When I said to my sister, *the Cone is yours, it belongs to you, I built it for you, and specifically in the center of the Kobernausser Forest,* I saw that the effect of the Cone on my sister was devastating. What followed was sheer horror, so Roithamer, nothing else, slow death, immersion in her sickness unto death, nothing else, from that moment forward everything led to her certain death (May 3).[10]

His suicide, the "ultimate correction" of his errors, concludes the novel. It has been widely misinterpreted as a mystical redemption of one sort or another, and especially of the Heideggerian variety. Roithamer hangs himself on the edge of a *Lichtung,* a clearing in the woods. The word belongs to the vocabulary of Heidegger's late works. However, one glance at Bernhard's treatment of Heidegger in *Old Masters* should lay to rest any suspicion that Bernhard intended to invoke Heideggerian philosophy.[11]

As in *Gargoyles* and *The Lime Works,* Bernhard introduces a narrator from outside the events. His task is to tell the story of Roithamer and his sister. The interlocutor is also an Austrian, like Roithamer a professor at Cambridge University in England but also a childhood companion of Roithamer and Höller. He is the witness figure whose task it is to impose some kind of form on his friend's miserable life. That form, of course, is the novel itself.

Bernhard resisted the term "novel" for his longer works. He preferred the more neutral "prose texts." Though the designation is moot, "novel" seems an apt enough idea if we understand it to mean the imposition of fictional form on the chaos of possible experience. Bernhard frames the Roithamer story by giving us as narrator the nervous and unhealthy Austrian mathematician from England. The frame is important because it supplies the archemedean point from which to view Roithamer's misery. The narrator does not moralize, he does not intervene, and he does not interpret. But he assembles the fragments of Roithamer's broken life and turns them into a narrative whole. He makes them accessible as aesthetic artifacts.

His artistic activity implies something about the *almost* transcendent character of art, even an art that takes despair and hopelessness as its theme. The narrator, as witness and artist, survives to tell the tale. He is nervous, in ill health, and certainly not an enviable specimen. But he has not capitulated to despair and death, which in Bernhard's universe is no mean accomplishment. Bernhard sheds light on the significance of such figures in an interview of 1983. In it he unexpectedly attempts to distinguish his pessimism from mere cynicism. "Even if all you see from your own perspective is ugliness and odium, every minute represents a growth of knowledge and experience. Even we at this very moment have a decisive advantage over those who died yesterday: knowing what's happened in the meantime."[12] It is a modest sort of wisdom, but not insignificant or unknown in the history of Austrian literature. "The situation may be hopeless," says a well-known piece of Austrian folk wisdom, "but it's not serious."

To put Bernhard in the context of an identifiable tradition of Austrian writing returns us to the example of Kafka. Bernhard's attitude belongs to the Kafkan tradition of ironic pessimism. "Is it possible," Kafka asks in a note to himself, "to think a disconsolate thought [etwas Untröstliches zu denken]? Or much more: to think a disconsolate thought without a whisper of consolation? A way out could be sought in insight itself as a form of consolation."[13] The narrator of *Correction*, and all of Bernhard's witness figures, are repositories for the consolations of insight. It is they who remain to contemplate the "corrections" of those who have consumed themselves in despair. Narrative is the form of their insight into the madness and calamity. The ultimate correction is not Roithamer's suicide, but is instead his friend's attempt to make sense of what was left behind.

NOTES

1. "Gemeinplätze, die Neueste Literatur betreffend," *Kursbuch* 15 (1968): 187–97; trans. by Michael Roloff as "Commonplaces on the Newest Literature," in Enzensberger, *The Consciousness Industry* (New York: Seabury, 1974) 83–94.
2. *Gathering Evidence* (New York: Knopf, 1985) 160.
3. Franz Kafka, *Hochzeitsvorbereitungen auf dem Lande und andere Prosa aus dem Nachlaß*, ed. Max Brod (Frankfurt am Main: Fischer, 1980) 53.
4. Alfred Barthofer, "Wittgenstein mit Maske," *Österreich in Geschichte und Literatur* 23 (1979): 186–207; Albrecht Weber, "Wittgensteins Gestalt und Theorie und ihre Wirkung im Werk Thomas Bernhards," *Österreich in Geschichte und Literatur* 25 (1981): 86–104.
5. *Correction* (New York: Knopf, 1979) 236.
6. Ria Endres, *Am Ende angekommen: Dargestellt am wahnhaften Dunkel der Männerporträts des Thomas Bernhard* (Frankfurt am Main: Fischer, 1980).
7. *Correction* 126.

8. *Correction* 265.
9. *Correction* 256.
10. *Correction* 267.
11. See chapter 5 below.
12. "Aveux et paradoxes de Thomas Bernhard," *Le Monde*, 7 Jan. 1983: 15.
13. Kafka, *Hochzeitsvorbereitungen* 53.

CHAPTER FOUR

The Spirit of Anarchy: Autobiographical Works

After the stormy success of *Frost* in 1963, Bernhard went on to establish his reputation not only as a superior stylist but also as a conspicuously prolific writer. He turned out a book or a play or both on his grandfather's old L. C. Smith typewriter almost every year for two and a half decades. At the same time Bernhard remained an exceedingly private man, almost a recluse. In 1965 he moved into a farmhouse in a rural village near Gmunden, in Upper Austria. His bad lungs had made city life an impossibility. He lived there in partial isolation—alone, without a telephone, and helped (reputedly) by a deaf-mute housekeeper—until his death in 1989. Bernhard never married, nor did he live with any permanent companion. His one close friend seems to have been an elderly woman, whom he thought of as his aunt, and who died in the early 1980s. Bernhard traveled often and owned other houses, but the farmhouse in Ohlsdorf remained his home.

The circumstances of such a life suggest a self-imposed exile. At least some of those who have had private dealings with Thomas Bernhard have reported him to have been an affable though retiring, even shy, man. He did not lead the public life of a conventional literary celebrity: no book reviews, essays, or lecture tours; he took no active part in political life (indeed, he nourished a lively contempt for politics and politicians); and he did nothing to encourage a positive image of himself in the media. Contrary to Austrian tradition, even his funeral was intensely private. Only immediate family were in attendance, and, in compliance with his wishes, no public announcement was made until after his burial in Vienna.

Perhaps the oddest thing about Bernhard's private life was the public image he chose to cultivate. He actively promoted the idea that he was an irascible misanthrope. The notorious letters to newspapers have already been discussed in chapter 1. But other aspects of his public life must be reviewed in this context as well. His interviews, for example, mostly show him to be a less than forthcoming subject:

HOFMANN: Is writing a kind of liberation for you or is it a protest?

THE SPIRIT OF ANARCHY

BERNHARD: No, I don't protest against anything.
HOFMANN: You're satisfied with everything?
BERNHARD: I'm satisfied with everything. Completely.
HOFMANN: Well then, why do you write?
BERNHARD: Probably because I'm so satisfied with myself and happy about everything.[1]

Though interviewing him was in general a frustrating assignment, Bernhard never failed to oblige his interlocutors by incanting the usual calumnies against Austria, politicians, doctors, the Burgtheater, the press, and his other favorite objects of scorn. But the tone remains facetious. He makes the impression of an actor playing a favorite role. In the same interview Bernhard even speaks of himself in the third person, as if he were talking about someone he happened to know and see occasionally ("The reporters come to me and not to him. And then I tell them a little bit about him").

The impression of play-acting is strengthened by Bernhard's "performances" at literary award ceremonies. His admirers showered him with literary honors.[2] Sometimes, early in his career, he was required to make acceptance speeches for his awards. On ceremonial occasions of this sort the feted literary star is expected to behave with the appropriate gratitude, dignity, and even modesty; he or she must offer a few well-chosen thoughts on the importance of literature for the health and well-being of civilized modernity. Thomas Bernhard, however, put into practice what his compatriot Peter Handke only imagined in a theater piece of 1966 called *Publikumsbeschimpfung (Insulting the Audience)*. In Handke's play the actors break the traditional compact between theatergoer and stage performer by verbally abusing the audience. Unwilling to accept dramatic convention at face value, Handke explodes that convention to see where the pieces fly.

The impact of Bernhard's acceptance speeches at award ceremonies is similar. Unwilling to accept at face value the conventions and assumptions of literary award-giving, Bernhard histrionically breaches the ceremonial etiquette of celebration with words of gloom, menace, and anarchy:

Honored Herr Minister, honored guests, there is nothing to praise, nothing to condemn, nothing to lament, but there is much that is *ridiculous;* everything is ridiculous if we but ponder *death.*

We Austrians populate a wound, we are frightened, we have a right to be frightened, in the background we already see, though indistinctly: the giants of fear. What we think is an *after*thought, what we feel is chaotic, what we are is unclear.

44

We need not feel ashamed, but we *are* nothing anyway and deserve nothing but chaos.

The comments are excerpts from a speech he made during a ceremony held in his honor. In the autobiographical novel *Wittgensteins Neffe* (1982; *Wittgenstein's Nephew, 1989*) Bernhard recounts the episode of 1967, when he was awarded the Austrian State Prize for Literature. He reports that after being forced to endure an error-ridden and even offensive speech about himself from an ill-informed minister of agriculture, it fell to him to say his piece:

> Just before the ceremony, in great haste and with the greatest reluctance, I had jotted down a few sentences, amounting to a small philosophical digression, the upshot of which was that man is a wretched creature and death a certainty. After I had delivered my speech, which lasted altogether no more than three minutes, the minister, who had understood nothing of what I had said, indignantly jumped up from his seat and shook his fist in my face. Snorting with rage, he called me a *curr* in front of the whole assembly and then left the chamber, slamming the glass door behind him with such force that it shattered into a thousand fragments.[3]

Bernhard's dramatic, even theatrical handling of award ceremonies reveals his odd sense of showmanship. He seemed to have a special persona that he put on for the occasion, like the new suit he bought for another award banquet described in *Wittgenstein's Nephew*. When that ceremony was over, he returned the suit to the store where he had bought it—as if to demonstrate that his public persona was a costume or mask to be discarded after use.

The comedy repeats itself. Bernhard recounts his version of yet another award ceremony, this one in 1971 when he received the Viennese Academy of Sciences' prestigious Grillparzer Prize. As Bernhard sees it, the Academy had simply marked him in the same way a dog marks a telephone pole: "It's true, I thought, they really have pissed on your head. They've done it to you again, just like they always do it to you. But you let them do it to you, I thought, and, what's worse, right in the Viennese Academy of Sciences." Evidently Bernhard never considered the option of declining all the awards that his admirers rained down on him.

But perhaps the best-known scandal that Bernhard stirred up was occasioned by his withdrawal from West Germany's Deutsche Akademie für Sprache und Dichtung (German Academy for Language and Literature). In

1970 the Academy awarded Bernhard its Georg Büchner Prize, probably the most prestigious of any German-language literary honor. As a holder of the Büchner Prize, Bernhard automatically became a member of the German Academy, an august body that includes the likes of Elias Canetti, Heinrich Böll, Jürgen Habermas, Christa Wolf, Hans-Georg Gadamer, Max Frisch, and many other luminaries of German letters. Suddenly in 1979, after seven years of quiescent membership, Bernhard became incensed when the Academy made former West German president Walter Scheel an honorary member. In protest he demonstratively withdrew from the German Academy and wrote a letter about it to the *Frankfurter Allgemeine Zeitung*. In it he decried Scheel's mediocrity and the venality of the Academy for having inducted the politician at all.[4] But the greater part of his animus was directed against the Academy itself, which he describes as a pretentious gathering of self-aggrandizing hypocrites. In the course of his animadversions he even sideswipes the practice of government subventions for writers, an institution from which he himself had been a beneficiary in needier times.

At best, Bernhard's case against Herr Scheel and the Academy is paltry. He seems mainly to have wanted a public quarrel with important people. These skirmishes, especially his feud with the German Academy, serve as an index to Bernhard's histrionic public persona. He was eager to present himself in an unfavorable light by gratuitously denouncing a popular figure and a distinguished institution. And oddly, at the same time he was making a public nuisance of himself, he guarded his own privacy with more than average zeal. Apart from his sequestered life style, the terms of his will illustrate a clear determination to conceal his private self from public view. Historically, most important writers have been willing to release their unfinished works, their diaries and correspondence after their death, at least after some time has elapsed. Not so Bernhard. His will forbids the scrutiny and publication of his private papers, correspondence, and even unpublished manuscripts, which reportedly include a partially completed novel entitled *Neufundland* (Newfoundland) and two plays, also presumably uncompleted. He went so far as to add to his will a special codicil to publicize his contempt for his compatriots. It prohibits any republication, performance, or recitation of his already published works in Austria for seventy years, the duration of his copyright. The will illustrates both sides of Bernhard's personality: the histrionic publicity seeker and the reticent private man. The solitary life in parochial Austria, without so much as a telephone to connect him with the outside, points toward a need for privacy. His public excesses, by contrast, suggest a man who yearns for public attention—even notoriety will do.

Though the evidence is circumstantial, I think it suggests that Bernhard, in public life, was constantly engaged in playing out a stylized version of himself. The coy interviews, the buffoonery of his letters to the press, and the theatrical posing at award ceremonies all point toward the deliberate cultivation of an image designed to conceal the inner man, or possibly to conceal the lack of a strong sense of inner self. In either case, the tension between Bernhard's public persona and private identity casts light on his motives for writing memoirs. In focusing attention on himself, Bernhard also focuses attention on his distinctly Austrian experience. By telling the story of his life, Bernhard simultaneously defines Austria itself from his special perspective. And his perspective—because of his national and international prominence as a writer—raises his life's story to a place of heightened importance.

Gathering Evidence: A Memoir

Between 1975 and 1982 Bernhard published the five separate books that contain his autobiography from birth to late teens. The English translation, entitled *Gathering Evidence: A Memoir* (1985), comprises all five in a single volume. Before proceeding with a discussion of these works, it should be noted that they do not reveal much about Bernhard's fiction or drama. He does not comment on his own work. But the memoirs do offer a context for interpretation. His pessimism is connected to his unhappy youth in Austria in obvious ways, but there are many other writers (Peter Handke, to name but one) whose wretched childhoods did not result in apocalyptic pessimism. There is no necessary link between the circumstances of his youth and his intellectual life. Bernhard's outlook is a matter of thoughtful choice. In his memoirs, as in his novels, he is the creator of his experience. He frames his own life with the sensibilities of a novelist, and he consciously establishes the mood that governs our response to it. Thus Bernhard's memoirs must be understood as an imaginative achievement in their own right.

His stated motive, taken from Montaigne, is simple: "I greedily long to make myself known, and I care not at what rate, provided it be truly."[5] His unstated motive, like that of any memoirist, is to give to his life intelligible form and meaning. The course of his thought and deeds must have a plot and a protagonist. The plot, as in his novels, takes impasse as its fundamental theme. The individual struggles against provincialism, ignorance, and malice only to be thwarted by death. Surprisingly, the primary protagonist is not Bernhard, but his grandfather, the novelist Johannes Freumbichler (1881–1949).

The grandfather is a ubiquitous presence in body and spirit throughout Bernhard's memoirs, a fixed point in an otherwise unstable set of outward circumstances. Strongly reminiscent of the narrators in his fiction, Bernhard casts himself as the witness to the travails of his protagonist. In the first book, *Ein Kind (A Child)*, which was the last to be written (1982), Bernhard recounts what he knows of his own illegitimate birth, his young mother's hardships and the difficulties she had in trying to control her precocious son. But the figure that dominates the narrative and the author's life is her father. He was an Austrian novelist of small reputation. The intervention of Carl Zuckmayer (whom Bernhard rather ungraciously refers to as "the so-called great writer") helped to gain him some public attention. His *Philomela Ellenhub: A Novel of Salzburg Peasant Life* earned the Austrian State Prize for Literature in 1937. Still, Freumbichler never managed to eke out a living as a professional writer.

Yet he invested all of his time and energy in his writing and reading. According to Bernhard's memoirs, Freumbichler was extraordinarily committed to the life of the mind. He did not hold any kind of job, so he depended on his lifelong companion, Anna Bernhard, their daughter, Herta Fabjan, and her husband, Emil Fabjan, to support him.[6] Bernhard hardly notices his grandfather's neglect of the family, but Freumbichler's excessive egoism and even his victimization of them is unmistakable. His mother, writes Bernhard, revered her father: "She worshiped a despot who was her beloved father, and who unconsciously and in keeping with his nature aimed at her annihilation." In spite of Bernhard's unreserved praise for his grandfather, what comes across to the reader is an image of a self-absorbed curmudgeon not unlike the protagonists of Bernhard's novels.[7] Bernhard once observed that his fictional protagonists are more or less modeled on his grandfather.[8] But the grandfather of the memoirs is too highly stylized, too much a literary character, to seem like a flesh-and-blood Austrian writer of the 1930s. Bernhard demonizes him for his own purposes. Freumbichler becomes larger than life: ruthlessly intellectual, uncompromising in his high standards, individualistic, almost infallible.

Interestingly, the novels help to understand the memoirs more than the memoirs help to understand the fiction. Bernhard's protagonists all suffer from an excess of intellect, one that brings destruction on them and their loved ones. If the grandfather is to be criticized, it is via the indirection of his fictional avatars. Freumbichler's fictional personae suffer for his real-life offenses. Yet Bernhard's admiration and love for his grandfather remain otherwise unqualified. He does not allow ambivalence to complicate the description of his surrogate father, the man who instilled in him his fundamental ideas and values.

In addition, Bernhard plainly modeled his own public persona on the image of his grandfather that he offers. "My grandfather loved chaos, he was an anarchist," boasts Thomas Bernhard, but then adds, "if only in spirit." Here he supplies the basic theme of his memoirs: the *spirit* of anarchy. The kind of anarchy that Bernhard loves is the kind he created in his speeches and letters and public battles. He aches to inject chaos into the mechanisms of Austrian bureaucracy and public institutions. Among his other writings the anti-art dramas he wrote for the Salzburg Festival are perhaps the most illuminating example. These works, which attack the assumptions that underlie the Salzburg Festival, will be taken up in chapter 6.

Bernhard's outrageous public appearances are exemplary of his anarchist strategy. He exploited his prestige as a writer to denounce the Austrian state, its artistic pretensions, its politicians. But his denunciations extend beyond the confines of Austria. With no respect for nuance, he indiscriminately repudiates all conventions, all institutions, all assumptions to the effect that the world is an orderly place in which fixed meanings and universal certainties can be discovered. Bernhard allows only one certainty: death; and all human doings—art, religion, politics—are nothing but useless maneuvers undertaken, consciously or not, with the aim of forgetting it.

With death as the one certainty in the world, life confronts Bernhard as an incomprehensible morass. He measures his own existence by the endless succession of suicides, fatal illnesses, and funerals that punctuate his autobiography. From early childhood on he sees himself poised on the edge of the abyss, vulnerable at every moment. *A Child* considers his life from birth until he begins boarding school in Salzburg. It is a childhood made up of episode after episode in which the untamable boy challenges the orderly, oppressive world of the powers that be: family, church, school. In *Die Ursache: Eine Andeutung (An Indication of the Cause)* Bernhard sketches out the causes of his early enmity with Salzburg. In particular he focuses attention on his clashes with a petty tyrant by the name of Grünkranz, his National Socialist schoolmaster. After the war a Catholic priest replaces

Grünkranz, a kindly man known to his pupils as Uncle Franz. But the priest was only a front; he had an enforcer, a prefect whose sadistic methods did not differ from those of the SA officer Grünkranz.

Bernhard never offers a reasoned analysis of Nazism as a historical or political phenomenon. But a more general critique is implicit in his withering assessment of Grünkranz and the spirit of wartime Salzburg. According to Bernhard, the city and its residents continue to be deformed by two basic forces: Nazism and Catholicism. National Socialism—but also Catholicism—epitomizes for him the pernicious, dehumanizing force of authoritarian order and control. But without discrimination or reservation Bernhard lumps Catholicism together with Nazism. Though he is plainly an implacable critic of National Socialism and all that it entails, Bernhard does not moralize about Nazism. He merely observes, contemplates what he saw, and refuses to forget it: the horror of corpses laid out in the streets, bombing raids, suicides, and the whole sorry spectacle of human nature in the grip of war and ideological illusions. It particularly rankles him that so many of his compatriots seem to have forgotten. "Whenever I come to the city today," writes Bernhard,

> I always take up the subject of those dreadful times, but people just shake their heads. In me these terrible experiences are just as present as if they had been only yesterday, when I enter Salzburg, sounds and smells that the city, as it seems, has expelled from its memory are immediately present, and when I talk to people here who are actually long-time residents of the city and must have experienced what I did, I talk to the most irritating, the most forgetful, the most ignorant people, it is as if I were speaking with one single offensive, mind-numbing ignorance.

Bernhard cannot forget, which suggests that his drama and fiction, like his memoirs, are a way of forcing people to see the informing anarchy of human nature, or at least to grasp his point of view.

His school experiences sent him scuttling as quickly as possible into the welcoming arms of chaos. In *Der Keller: Eine Entziehung (The Cellar: An Escape)* Bernhard tells the story of how at sixteen years of age he suddenly gave up the idea of a conventional *Gymnasium* education and the secure future it offered. On his way to school one morning he happened to pass the local employment agency. He went in and found a spot as a grocer's apprentice, intentionally selecting a shop located in a cellar in Salzburg's grimmest, most impoverished and disorderly district, a section of town called the Scherzhauserfeld Settlement. In so doing Bernhard actively traded the deadening order and authority of "the learning machine" for the sad but more human surroundings of a ghetto. Bernhard claims that this phase of his life among the Austrian outcastes was his happiest. Among other things it meant a partial escape from National Socialism:

> It is telling that in the Scherzhauserfeld Settlement there were no National Socialists, but even their opposition to Nazidom did nothing to better their lot after the war. . . . A few communists and what the National Socialists designated as *asocial elements* were exterminated by the Nazis, also in the Scherzhauserfeld Settlement, from among the *Scherzhauserfeld rabble,* as they believed and dared to put it then and once again dare to put it today, the Nazis picked out what they called the *worst of the lot* and sent them to be gassed or otherwise annihilated. Once again the minority lives in fear. But anyone who says so is sure to be slandered and accused of lying.

To be an outcaste means exclusion from the social and political order. It also means being left to determine one's own self. Bernhard avers that he first felt free to be himself in the Scherzhauserfeld Settlement. No one imposed any grand order on his life; he felt no compulsion to live up to the expectations of others or to plan for his future.

Toward the end of *The Cellar* he sums up his objections to order and authority: "Theories alone maim us—that is abundantly clear—philosophies and the various fields of knowledge as a whole, whose useless insights get in the way of clarity." Truth is a personal matter, one that is felt and difficult, if not impossible, to communicate. Bernhard's memoirs, like his fiction and drama, are predicated on the assumption that language and art can only approximate truth. Truth is elusive and cannot be captured with certainty and finality. It is mutable and so has a different look as perspectives vary. In this, as in so much else, Bernhard is one of Kafka's legitimate heirs. To offer two among many possible examples, Kafka writes: "It is difficult to tell the truth, for—even though there is only one—it is living and therefore has a lively face";[9] "Truth is indivisible, therefore cannot recognize itself; whoever wants to recognize it has to be a lie."[10] Bernhard's premises are virtually the same: "The truth that we know is logically the lie that, insofar as we cannot circumvent it, is the truth. What is being described here [in *The Cellar*] is the truth yet still not the truth because it cannot be the truth." Though Bernhard elsewhere, especially in interviews, claims that he only reports the facts, here he more circumspectly sets the limits of his art. He aims for the truth, presumably, by overstatement. He attempts to provoke us into a contemplation of his experience of the world and not into an objective grasp of spiritual truth or historical fact except by oblique approximation.

Bernhard's anarchism, then, shapes many aspects of his life: art and language dwell in the chaos of self-conscious untruth; philosophy and theory mutilate the soul; politics and religion are untruth of the most mind-destroying variety. Even personally Bernhard felt most alive in the relative anarchy of the Scherzhauserfeld Settlement. He prefers anarchy to order not because it is beneficial to himself or anybody else. He prefers it simply because he believes that chaos is the truest, most natural arrangement of human affairs. Order stultifies and enslaves by turning out mass-produced nonindividuals.

The lack of nuance is characteristic. But Bernhard speaks only for himself. Self-reliance and human dignity do not necessarily unfold under the circumstance of anarchy. Still, Bernhard offers it as the ground in which they might best take root—or at least did in his case. And what took root during Bernhard's apprenticeship in the grocer's cellar shop was an abiding commitment to music. He began taking voice lessons (bass) after hours and developed a serious interest in music theory as well. But the decisive point for him was not intrinsic to the music itself. What made the turn to music a watershed in his life was the simple fact that he chose it voluntarily: "Of my own free will: that was the main thing."

Yet as attractive as anarchy must have been to him, even a soul as sturdy as Bernhard's cannot withstand permanent chaos. The musical path he had chosen represented for him an almost unshakable source of pleasure and self-assurance, but only *almost*. At a time when Bernhard's spirits were higher than they had ever been, and when he had organized his life into a more or less orderly whole, chaos unexpectedly showed its ugly side—as if to bring him back to his senses. He became deathly ill in January of 1949, a few days before his eighteenth birthday. In *Der Atem: Eine Entscheidung* (*Breath: A Decision*) Bernhard recounts his initial bout with mortal illness. First his beloved grandfather was hospitalized with a condition that later killed him. Shortly thereafter Bernhard too had to be hospitalized with a case of pleurisy so severe that his doctors gave him up for dead. Grandfather and grandson were both engaged at the same time in a literal struggle against death; only Bernhard survived.

The story of his experiences in the hospital's ghoulish ward for terminal cases, comprising almost exclusively very old men and staffed with icily efficient nuns, is one of Bernhard's most gripping narratives. In the overall picture that he presents of himself in his memoirs, the "death ward" section of *Breath: A Decision* gives the clearest image of his powerful self-reliance. At the crucial moment, after extreme unction had already been administered to him, and as he was listening to the death rattle of the man in the bed next to him, Bernhard gathered his inner forces for one last push:

> I wanted to *live,* all else meant nothing. *To live,* and by that I meant living my own life, *in a way and as long as I wanted.* That was no oath, that was something decided by the one they had given up for dead, and at the very moment in which the man next to him had ceased to breathe. That night, at the decisive moment, I decided between two paths.

His inner strength prevailed for the moment, and Bernhard managed a recovery as arduous as it was gradual. The death of his grandfather was a devastating blow, but it also liberated his sense of self and individuality: "ich hatte immer nur *ich* werden wollen," he always had only wanted to become who he was. The theme of evolving a self dominates the memoirs as much as it dominates the fiction. For instance, *Frost* offers the story of a young man attracted to an older, highly individualistic artist not unlike old Freumbichler. Though the novel concentrates on Strauch, it is no less the story of the young man's need to break away from an old man in order to become himself. The pattern of *Gargoyles* does not differ significantly.

When Bernhard had recovered sufficiently to be moved, his doctors sent him to what they called a convalescent home. It was set in the mountains near Großgmain on the Bavarian border, but it turned out to be part convalescent home and part hospice. Worse yet, the unlucky teen-ager found himself largely in the company of tuberculosis patients. Naturally Bernhard contracted tuberculosis and soon found himself pitched once again into a battle for his life.

The description of the next confrontation with death, which makes up the final volume of his memoirs, *Die Kälte: Eine Isolation* (*In the Cold*), is even more pitiless than that of the death ward. The doctors moved Bernhard, still an eighteen-year-old, to Grafenhof, a sanatorium that specialized in the treatment of TB. At first they falsely diagnosed his case as benign and even pronounced him cured. But the disease soon broke out in its full virulence, whereupon he was transferred back to the hospital in Salzburg for a series of gruesome (and frequently bungled) treatments that involved puncturing his abdomen and pumping him up with air. While he was in the hospital there, he lost his mother at a time when they were learning to understand each other. At the age of forty-six she died a terribly painful death of uterine cancer.

Soon Bernhard found himself in Grafenhof again. Here he witnessed what amounted to a society of living corpses. They dragged their wasted bodies through each new day, always carrying with them their sputum jars of brown glass, and vying with one another to hack up ever greater quantities of the nauseating fluids produced by their broken lungs. The atmosphere of the place mesmerized Bernhard, who found himself succumbing to its morbid spirit. He was losing his recently renewed appetite for life, not quite able to rally himself for the necessary battle.

Perhaps what roused him was the discovery of someone to hate. The director of the sanatorium was a former Nazi, a petty tyrant whom Bernhard characterizes as dim-witted and sadistic. The obvious parallel must be drawn to Bernhard's other antagonists, and in particular to Grünkranz, the headmaster of his old boarding school. The sanatorium, like his old school, seemed like a penitentiary to him, designed not for healing but for robbing him of his individuality. Once again he finds himself in a large, impersonal ward; the head physician, fanatically obsessed with power, refused even to answer Bernhard's questions about his own case; patients were housed and even nourished according to their caste in Austrian society. Outrageously, all the patients simply accommodated themselves to the order of things and accepted what Bernhard calls the law of Grafenhof.

The consequence of the many personal humiliations at Grafenhof was revolt: "I rebelled more violently than ever against Grafenhof and its laws, against inevitability!" The anarchist Bernhard revolts against the demeaning regimentation of the sanatorium, precisely as he rebelled against the order of his family, of his school, against organized religion, and on and on. His later rebellions, like the one against the German Academy of Language and Literature, belong in the same category of self-assertion and self-preservation. His foremost aims were survival and self-definition.

Rebellion in the interest of shaping individuality is the theme that anchors his memoirs. The act of writing itself was no doubt a similar fortification of self for Thomas Bernhard, a damaged soul. He is settling old scores by describing them, fairly or unfairly. In so doing he continued to define himself as the individual who said *No!* to an order that was oppressive, mendacious, or simply wrong.

His most notorious settling of old scores is the more or less autobiographical novel of 1984, *Holzfällen: Eine Erregung* (*Woodcutters*).[11] Set in the 1980s, it is told from the perspective of a narrator who is also a character in the story and who also strongly resembles Thomas Bernhard. He is a writer attending a dinner party with other successful artists and intellectuals from the generation of the 50s, people he has not seen for twenty years. The hosts and guests of the dinner are identifiable as Bernhard's associates and supporters from the beginning of his career. In the book Bernhard takes up his "observer's post" (a favorite conceit of his from the memoirs) and proceeds to spin out a blistering satire. It is directed against his former associates who, in his view, have sacrificed their artistic and moral integrity for money and status in the fishbowl of intellectually chic Viennese society. A main theme is the Austrian artist's relation to the state as a principal source of income (and prestige) through its many subventions, prizes, and cultural institutions:

> Being an artist in Austria usually means truckling to the state, no matter which, and then allowing yourself to be supported by it for a lifetime. The road of artistry in Austria is one that is phony, mean-spirited, and opportunistic; it is paved with state fellowships and prizes, with honors and medals, and it ends in a prestigious grave in the Central Cemetery.

The impudent book struck a nerve in Austrian cultural life. A measure of its embarrassing truth may well be the flap it incited. One of the book's real-life prototypes, a composer named Gerhard Lampersberg, for whom Bernhard had written librettos in the late 50s, recognized himself in the drunken has-been Auersberger. Not without reason Lampersberg (a "lecherous devourer of writers") felt he had been used badly by a writer who had been his protégé. The incensed composer was influential enough to stop the book's sale for several weeks in Austria.[12]

In *Woodcutters,* as in the memoirs, Bernhard launches an all-out verbal assault against the dehumanizing force of conformism. The artistic establishment of Vienna and the regime of Grafenhof differ only in degree. What they share in his mind is a distinctly Austrian character. Bernhard tirelessly heaps abuse on his homeland at every opportunity, fairly and unfairly. His detractors in Austria always point out that he himself benefited from government prizes and subventions; that many suffered more than he did; that his complaints and accusations are grossly exaggerated—all of which is true enough. However, when reading Bernhard's memoirs and fiction—both of which rest on his talent for hyperbole and verbal music—a wider perspective is necessary.

In his memoirs Bernhard draws our attention above all to a world in which norms and certainties—family, religion, homeland, philosophy, art, science, and language—do not hold. A fatherless child, largely rejected by his mother (she sent him every month to pick up his own tiny relief check of five marks with the cutting remark "so that you see what you're worth"), raised outside of religion, unable to gain a footing in school, Bernhard had very little to support the child's fragile ego. He was master of nothing, not even his own body, as his uncontrollable bedwetting demonstrated. As if his problem were not humiliating enough already, his mother made certain that his incontinence was a matter of common knowledge in their neighborhood by displaying his stained bedsheet. "Every day my mother hoisted the banner of my disgrace. When I would come home from school, shoulders hunched, there it was, flapping in the wind, showing everyone what I was."

Significantly, Bernhard enjoyed a certain amount of prestige in school as an athlete, and as an apprentice he forgot his misery in blissfully hard physical labor. All teen-agers believe they are immortal, and to Bernhard his body must have seemed the last refuge of self. But it was hard work that broke his health. Unloading potatoes during January of 1949, when he suffered from a high fever, Bernhard began his lifelong struggle with disease. If his body seemed to him the one certainty in an otherwise unreliable world, his experience of disease and medical science soon disabused him of the illusion. Yet Bernhard persevered, consciously deciding for his own life and dignity. As a writer he held to his pain, used it intellectually and imaginatively as a moral indicator and as the last refuge of personal identity. When his body failed, Bernhard clung to music in Grafenhof, and it was there that he discovered literature, which became the vehicle of defining and developing the sense of self that had never before found a place to take root. "I immersed myself in Verlaine and Trakl, and I read *The Demons* by Dostoyevsky. . . . The monstrousness of *The Demons* made me strong, showed me a way, told me that I was on the right track, the one that led *out.*" As a writer Bernhard stayed on the monstrous track, and it served him well. But he remained careful never to celebrate art, music, and literature as redemptive. The imaginative intellect does not transcend the world's uncertainties; it merely holds them at bay.

NOTES

1. From Bernhard's final interview, "Letzte Worte aus der Einsamkeit," *Der Spiegel,* 29 Jan. 1990: 162–63.

2. The Julius Campe Prize, 1964; Bremen Prize, 1965; the Austrian State Prize for Literature, 1967; Presentation of the Culture Circle of the Federated League of German Industry,

1967; Anton Wildgans Prize of the Austrian Industrialists' Association, 1968; the Georg Büchner Prize, 1970; the Grillparzer Prize, 1972; the Franz Theodor Csokor Prize of the Austrian PEN Club, 1972; the Adolf Grimme Prize, 1972; the Hannover Dramatists Prize, 1974; the Prix Séguier, 1974; Literature Prize of the Austrian Chamber of Commerce, 1976; the Premio Prato, 1982; the Premio Modello, 1983; and the Prix Medicis, 1988.

3. For the text of Bernhard's speech (as well as another that he was not allowed to present) see "Die Wahrheit und dem Tod auf der Spur: Zwei Reden," *Neues Forum* 173 (1968): 347–49; for an external account of the episode see Josef Donnenberg, "Thomas Bernhard und Österreich," *Österreich in Geschichte und Literatur* 14 (1970): 237–51.

4. "Zu meinem Austritt," *Frankfurter Allgemeine Zeitung*, 7 Dec. 1979: 25.

5. The translation comprises *Die Ursache* (1975); *Der Keller* (1976); *Der Atem* (1978); *Die Kälte* (1981); and *Ein Kind* (1982); all five memoirs were published by Salzburg's Residenz Verlag.

6. Thomas bears the last name Bernhard because his mother was Freumbichler's illegitimate child by Anna Bernhard. Freumbichler married Anna in 1938, after they had already spent thirty-four years together. Herta Bernhard became Herta Fabjan when she married Emil Fabjan in 1935. Fabjan, whom Bernhard slightly refers to by the technical term *Vormund* (legal guardian), plays no significant role in the memoirs. Bernhard is vague on many such details, but Caroline Markolin has worked out many of them in her useful book *Die Großväter sind die Lehrer: Johannes Freumbichler und sein Enkel Thomas Bernhard* (Salzburg: Otto Müller, 1988).

7. Particularly as Bernhard presents him in *The Cellar*: "Especially against women—against his wife, against my mother, his daughter—he could proceed with a virtually annihilating harshness and severity."

8. "Drei Tage," *Der Italiener* (Salzburg: Residenz, 1971).

9. Franz Kafka, *Briefe an Milena*, ed. Willy Haas (Frankfurt am Main: Fischer Taschenbuch, 1966) 54.

10. Franz Kafka, *Hochzeitsvorbereitungen auf dem Lande*, ed. Max Brod (Frankfurt am Main: Fischer Taschenbuch, 1980) 36.

11. Oddly, this novel has been translated twice, first by Ewald Osers as *Cutting Timber* (London: Quartet, 1985) and then by David McLintock as *Woodcutters* (New York: Knopf, 1987).

12. For a useful documentation of the day-by-day antics of the dramatis personae see Eva Schindlecker, "Thomas Bernhard *Holzfällen:* Dokumentation eines österreichischen Literaturskandals," *Statt Bernhard*, ed. Wendelin Schmidt-Dengler and Martin Huber (Vienna: Edition S, 1987) 13–58.

CHAPTER FIVE

The Hidden Wound:
Old Masters and *Auslöschung*

By the 1980s Thomas Bernhard had become one of the German-speaking world's best known, most celebrated, most notorious authors. He had won most of the major awards that were to be had. His earnings from his books and plays were substantial. Yet all his success was the result of writing based on the premise that life is a hopeless venture. Consequently, worldly triumph must have been something of a philosophical problem for this most severe of literary pessimists.

Bernhard dealt with the paradox in part by denigrating the honors that his peers accorded him. His acrimonious withdrawal from the German Academy, discussed in chapter 4, is evidence enough of his intention to remain an outsider. Rejecting the trappings of prestige and power is one way of keeping in touch with the basal humanity from which success might otherwise estrange him. He could have rested on the laurels of his prosperity and the flattery of his admirers, but he did not; rather, he continued to act out the attitude that shaped his fiction.

He defined himself and his position clearly in his memoirs: he was born among the pariahs of society in Austria, a country in which he and his family were made to suffer. Because his writing stems from his personal experience in Austria, he would not betray the truth of that experience by conforming to Austria's cult of artistic celebrity. The Salzburg plays of the 1970s, which will be taken up in the next chapter, document his contempt for the social prestige of high art. Bernhard holds fast to the idea that art should offer a critical perspective uncompromised by debts to institutions. It would be amusing to imagine what might transpire if Bernhard, like so many of his American colleagues, were the holder of an academic chair in a university. But such a turn of events is inconceivable, and not just because Austrian universities do not have "creative writing" programs. Bernhard's work is imaginable only outside institutional boundaries. He relentlessly describes the world from his highly individualistic point of view. If there is a paradox in his Austrian success, it is that he has been so popular in a society geared to the conformist values of the culture industry, and not that he has been willing to accept success.

Bernhard had little choice in the matter of accepting or not accepting success. In any case, the apparent paradox of his material success melts away when viewed from the perspective of his lifetime of disease and his early death. He lost his health permanently when he was in his teens. Moreover, he lost it needlessly. He contracted tuberculosis because he was sent to convalesce from pleurisy at a sanatorium that housed TB patients. At the same time he lost his grandfather because an obstructed bladder was misdiagnosed as a tumor. And he lost his mother because her doctors diagnosed her uterine cancer too late. Bernhard's later success as a writer could not change or transcend any of this.

What remains to be examined, then, is the specific place of art in his imagination. Even though Bernhard did not conform to the image of the German artist-intellectual in either of its conventional varieties (the one being politically and socially committed, the other being an ivory tower mandarin), he seems to have realized that the nimbus of transcendence somehow clings to his fiction and drama. Even the darkest, most rancorous despair and rage seem to transcend or even ennoble animal suffering when sublimated by high imagination into word and music. The work that deals most directly with Bernhard's ambivalent feelings about art as a form of transcendence is a novel entitled *Alte Meister* (1985; *Old Masters*, 1989).

Old Masters

The structure of *Old Masters* conforms to Bernhard's long-standing preference for a witness who reports on the views and opinions of the main protagonist. Atzbacher, a young Viennese intellectual, reports on his friend Reger, an eighty-two-year-old man of rarefied aesthetic knowledge and sensibilities. For over three decades Reger—a free-lance intellectual who reports on music from Vienna to the London *Times*—has visited the Art Historical Museum every other day. It is his custom always to sit in the Bordone Room on a settee in front of Tintoretto's *Man with a White Beard*. There he thinks and reads, and sometimes lectures Atzbacher on music, art, and literature. He has devoted his entire life to understanding art.

What links *Old Masters* to *Correction* and other earlier novels, apart from its basic format, is once again the symbolic idea of femininity as a propagation of the self. This time the idea is embodied in a wife and a sister, separately. Reger had a sister, but she was not destined for survival. She died of heart failure at the age of nineteen on their father's fifty-ninth birthday and amidst the mother's frenzied preparations for a birthday party. Reger describes it as an escape from their tyrannical parents, who, as ever, represent a spiritually oppressive Austria. The dead sister belongs to the list of silent women who, since the death of Strauch's sister in *Frost*, prove unable to survive in the atmosphere of modernity, an atmosphere that Reger characterizes as thoroughly brutalized. It should be mentioned in passing that the brief novellas *Ja* (Yes, 1978) and *Beton* (1982; *Concrete*, 1984) sympathetically, but without the least trace of sentimentality, explore the fates of brutalized women.

Unlike the destructive men who dominate most of Bernhard's novels, Reger is aware of his need for the civilizing presence of woman. He recovers the influence of his lost sister in the influence of his wife. For more than forty years Reger was a happily married man, tenderly devoted to her. She always accompanied him on his visits to the Tintoretto painting; in fact, they met in the Bordone Room in front of the *Man with a White Beard*. Like the other lost sisters and wives, she represents an Austria that has disappeared forever. It is she who loves and owns works by the great twentieth-century Austrians: Loos and Otto Wagner, Klimt and Schiele; it is she who loves Vienna. But Reger lost her, when at the age of eighty-two she died of a fall in front of Vienna's Art Historical Museum (the city failed to salt the walk properly on an icy day). Now that Reger has been alone for the nine years since her death, he is left to contemplate the novel's eponymous old masters of painting, music, literature, and philosophy.

His reflections make up the greater part of *Old Masters*, which bears the subtitle "A Comedy." It is the funniest of Bernhard's longer "prose texts," as he liked to call them, and one of his most deft prose performances. Its two most scalding passages are directed against Adalbert Stifter, the much celebrated novelist of nineteenth-century Austria, and Martin Heidegger, the old master of twentieth-century philosophy. In a lengthy tirade against Stifter (but directed mainly against the current nostalgia for Habsburg culture that is in vogue among Austrian intellectuals and often expressed as a demonstrative fondness for Stifter's work) Reger makes the novelist out to be a small-time bungler and dilettante. But he saves his most venomous denunciations for Heidegger and the cult of folksy simplicity that has formed around the former Nazi and his philosophy of Being. A brief excerpt will give the flavor of the whole:

I have seen a series of photographs that a supremely talented woman photographer made of Heidegger, who in all of them looks like an obese staff officer in retirement, Reger said, and I'll show them to you one of these days; in the photographs Heidegger is just climbing out of bed, or Heidegger is climbing into bed, or Heidegger is sleeping, or waking up, putting on his underpants, slipping into his socks, taking a sip of grape juice, stepping out of his log cabin and gazing into the horizon, whittling his walking stick, putting on his cap, taking off his cap, holding his cap in his hands, spreading his legs, raising his head, lowering his head, putting his right hand in his wife's left hand while his wife is putting her left hand in his right hand, walking in front of his house, walking behind his house, walking toward his house, walking away from his house, reading, eating, spooning his soup, slicing off a piece of bread (baked by him), opening a book (written by him), closing a book (written by him), bending down, straightening up, and so on, Reger said. Enough to make you puke.[1]

Reger is obsessed with these and other so-called old masters. He sees his main task as one of critique in the corrosive sense. He seeks to discover the "grave flaw" hidden in every masterwork of painting, of music, or of literature. "Not only does perfection threaten without respite to annihilate us, it also annihilates everything that hangs on these walls that goes under the name of *masterpiece*. . . . Only when we repeatedly discover that perfection and the whole do not exist does the continuation of life become a possibility."

The theme of perfection is an old one for Bernhard. His protagonists have all been perfectionists of one sort or another, driven, often fatally, by the idea of perfecting their life's work: building the perfect house (*Correction*), writing the absolutely definitive study of hearing (*The Lime Works*) or of Mendelssohn-Bartholdy (*Concrete*) or of physiognomy (*Die Billigesser* [*The Cheap-Eaters*]), a perfect performance of Schubert's *Trout Quintet* (*The Force of Habit*), and others.

In an obvious way the need for perfection can make life unbearable. Perhaps the most revealing treatment of the theme occurs in his novel of 1983 *Der Untergeher* (Going Under). In it Bernhard invents two fictional colleagues for Glenn Gould. Like Wittgenstein, the reclusive piano virtuoso Gould lived the kind of life that Bernhard admired. He was a reclusive genius who followed the track of his own creative genius. Like Bernhard, Gould developed a unique style from his own inner resources. In addition, Gould succumbed in 1982 to what might be called a Thomas Bernhard death. At the youthful age of fifty-one and at the height of his artistic powers, Gould died suddenly and unexpectedly of a stroke. In the Thomas Bernhard scheme of things, this is precisely the right moment. Gould, however, is not the protagonist of the novel. The main protagonist is a man named Wertheimer.

Together with the narrator and Glenn Gould, Wertheimer studied piano under Horowitz in Salzburg during the early 50s. Whereas Gould developed into the great Bach interpreter, Wertheimer and the narrator found themselves unable to measure up to the standards of perfection set by their friend. It is Gould who dubs Wertheimer an *Untergeher*, a man destined to be overwhelmed by life. And indeed, Wertheimer's sense of failure drives him to suicide. He hangs himself from a tree in front of the home of his sister, to whom he was peculiarly attached. It is significant that Wertheimer reverses the brother-sister configuration of *The Lime Works* and *Correction*. In *Der Untergeher* the beloved sister chooses life and its manifold uncertainties for herself, escape from her demented brother. Rather than destroying her, as Konrad and Roithamer did, Wertheimer simply kills himself—spitefully, though, in front of her house. The brother seeks certainty and eternity in his relationship to her and in his quest for artistic perfection. Technical virtuosity, perfection of technique, takes on connotations of a living death. Gould, who has perfected his technique, dies while performing his renowned Goldberg Variations; Wertheimer, unable to perfect his technique (or bind his sister to him), commits suicide. In either case perfection means death.

Returning to *Old Masters* we find a Bernhard protagonist who has seen through the murderous claims of artistic perfection. Tintoretto's *Man with a White Beard* embodies for Reger all that is false and treacherous in great art: the utopian promise of transcendence, of human nobility, of perfection. However, he does not deny art its place in his life; indeed, since the loss of his wife only the detested old masters sustain him. But he resists them, seeks that which is imperfect in them, which is to say that he seeks the most human part of all. Reger survives by continually rediscovering the flawed element in seeming perfection. It is not much of an existence, as he freely admits, but it enables him to carry on. Reger lives as if he were motivated by Nietzsche's famous dictum: "We have art that we may not perish of the truth." He means that illusion and self-deception alone offer relief; true redemption is out of the question.

Reger's point, strikingly similar to Nietzsche's, is that high art inevitably appeals to a basic human need for mystification and escape. But when art and literature are put to the test—as when measured against the animal pain of a loved one's death—even great art seems paltry:

> We believe we can cling to Shakespeare or Kant, but it's not true, Shakespeare and Kant and all the others whom in the course of a lifetime we stylize as the so-called great minds leave us stranded at the moment we need them most, so Reger, they are no solution and they are no consolation; suddenly they are only repulsive and alien, everything that the so-called great minds and significant thinkers thought and then wrote leaves us unimpressed, so Reger.

Again Reger speaks in a way that recalls Nietzsche. In *Beyond Good and Evil* (section 269) Nietzsche declares that "the great poets" conceal from themselves their damaged souls. It is an inner wound, he argues, that leads great artists to take revenge for

> some inner desecration, often seeking oblivion in lofty flight from their all-too-faithful memories, often lost in muck and almost in love with it until, like foxfire in the bogs, they *mimic* the stars (whereupon the masses will likely call them idealists), often caught up in a long struggle against a nausea, against a ghostlike skepticism that always comes back to haunt them and chills them and makes them long for hymns of praise and eager to lap up "faith in itself" from the hands of intoxicated flatterers. Oh what a *torture* all these great artists and these altogether higher men are, what a torture to him who has guessed their true nature!

Nietzsche may sound like Freud here, but the repressed "inner desecration" is not necessarily sexual. Nietzsche leaves open a variety of hidden wounds as potential motives for self-deception. He speaks only of the *Schlamm*, the nauseating mire and muck of existence. In Bernhard, and possibly in Nietzsche too, the wound is ultimately the knowledge of death, the discovery of human finitude. Reger has made the bleak discovery, and it has led him to understand the repressive, deceptive nature of masterpieces and of the old masters.

Nietzsche also offers another clue to the deeper nature of Bernhard's undertaking. There is an inner desecration that motivates Bernhard too, for Bernhard (and even Reger) are old masters in their own right. The hidden wound that makes Bernhard's writing so vivid and compelling is, I think, not primarily the psychic wounds of the boy he describes in his memoirs. They are themselves symptomatic of a deeper wound, a collective one that includes Bernhard but also transcends him. It is Austrian history. In no work of his fiction is this trauma so close to the surface as in his final novel *Auslöschung: Ein Zerfall* (Obliteration: A Disintegration, 1986).

Auslöschung

"We populate a wound," Bernhard once said to an Austrian audience. In a clear sense his life's work probes the wound of Austrian history. It is one long assault on Austrian repression, self-satisfaction, and complacency. Yet Bernhard seldom wrote or discussed history except as he experienced it personally. History is not an abstract reflection on ideas and events, but is instead personal, even bodily, experience. Bernhard recalls the animal terror of being packed into badly ventilated bomb shelters; he remembers corpses on the streets of Salzburg and his experiences with the Nazi schoolmasters and youth organizations. The tone he sets in his memoirs is also carried out in the fiction: history reverts to ontology.

So Bernhard never wrote historical novels in the ordinary sense. But his imagination is historical in that it gives significant form to the spiritual consequences of history. *Auslöschung* is a case in point. Its protagonist is Franz-Josef Murau, a man whose first name is a historical allusion that marks him as an heir to Old Austria's fate: decline, failure, and obliteration. Murau, a rootless intellectual living in Rome, has received a telegram informing him that his mother, father, and older brother have been killed in an accident. He is now the only surviving son, a reluctant heir to the vast and ancient Austrian estate known as Wolfsegg. The novel, Bernhard's longest, consists of his written reflections as he prepares to leave Rome, then during his brief stay for the funeral at Wolfsegg with his two repellent sisters, and finally when he returns to Rome and suddenly dies.

The archetypical Thomas Bernhard plot is by now so familiar that it hardly needs restating. The estate, like Austria itself, was once grand and mighty. But its legacy has been squandered by unworthy heirs. In other books Bernhard presents the heirs as simply and inexplicably degenerate. In *Auslöschung* he makes it plain that National Socialism is the particular form of modern Austrian degeneration, the disease from which no recovery is possible. The metaphor is precise, for disease—the exemplary image of Bernhardian destruction—is always fraught with an otherwise inexplicable dimension of moral justification about it in his prose. Outwardly he portrays disease and incest, madness and death, as meaningless features of a meaningless universe. Yet the moral logic of his imagery is unmistakable. He consistently deploys the metaphorics of sickness and degeneration in such a way that a pattern gradually emerges and allows the meaning to assert itself. *Disease is an expression of Bernhard's historically rooted moral pessimism.* Among other things he uses it to name the inner truth of National Socialism and its debilitating consequences in Austria and elsewhere. Bernhard has turned the myth of blood and soil against itself.

As Franz-Josef Murau ponders the life to which he was born and which he has always struggled against, we learn that his parents were unrepentant Nazis. The scars of Nazism are the books' basic theme; as Murau puts it in his vast monologue, the Nazi era was

> the most repulsive era ever experienced at Wolfsegg, I said to Gambetti, it debased Wolfsegg, it killed Wolfsegg, it was a time never, ever to be cloaked in silence or glossed over because it is the truth. When I tell you that my father invited Nazi VIPs to Wolfsegg only because my mother insisted on it, it still sends a shiver down my spine. That it was possible for the local storm troopers to come into the courtyard shrieking *Heil Hitler*! No doubt my father turned a profit on the Nazis. And when they were gone he got off scot free, absolutely scot free. Without missing a beat he even became the grand gentleman for everyone around after the war. Of his own free will he put our smaller villa at the Nazis' disposal for their meetings, I know, my mother never had to encourage him to do it. The Hitler Youth did their arts and crafts in our smaller villa and learned their dimwitted Nazi songs there. Year-in and year-out the swastika flag waved above the smaller villa until my mother hauled it down, tattered and faded, a few hours before the Americans arrived.

Though Murau is a lucid critic of his family history, he is also its captive. He changed cultures and languages in an attempt to free himself of his own tainted blood, but there is no escape from genetic inheritance. Now his parents and elder brother have died in a traffic accident, propelling him to an unwanted position as family head.

When Murau arrives at Wolfsegg, he is gripped with a morbid desire to open his mother's closed coffin in order to look at her corpse, which was horribly mutilated in the accident. The awful desire to see her disfigured, decapitated body figures significantly in the overall logic of the novel. Bernhard's oft-avowed intention as a writer is to reveal the truth, no matter how distressing. The principal theme of *Auslöschung* is the maiming of Austria. Murau's desire to see his mother as she is, so to speak, reflects the Bernhardian obsession with unsightly moral truths about Austria: its tradition of anti-semitism, its enthusiasm for Nazism. And the fact that it is the mother who has been mangled, and not the father or brother, also fits into the larger picture of Bernhard's feminine characters.

In earlier chapters of this study I have tried to show that there is a class of oppressed female characters in Bernhard's fiction who represent certain "feminine" virtues: silent wholeness, passivity, rootedness in family, and the like. These figures are destroyed by their male counterparts, usually an excessively intellectual husband or brother (or sometimes both in one). Often the brother-sister relationship is incestuous. As in William Faulkner's vision of the degeneration of the American South since the Civil War, Bernhard's postwar Austria is rife with symbolic incest. It suggests a perverted world turned inward on itself, narcissistically fixated on its own past, unable to move into the future with vigor and confidence. *The Lime Works, Correction,* and *Eve of Retirement* as well as other works capitalize on the idea of sibling incest.

But there is another class of women characters, beginning with the slovenly innkeeper's wife in *Frost*. These women are man-devouring harridans. Most often they are mothers—for instance, Roithamer's mother in *Correction*—who have risen from the lowest, most brutal element of Austrian society to become wives of landed gentlemen of ancient family. It is they, and their repulsive daughters, who taint the bloodline. In Bernhard's peculiar genetics of national collapse, these grasping women are the destroyers of Austria. They dominate the weaker, world-weary men they marry, produce the vilest of offspring, and attempt to control the lives of those around them. It is they who determine the quality of modern "family life," Bernhard's metaphor for national life. Murau's mother (and his two silly sisters) belong to this genre of imaginary female demon. The role of the "good sister" belongs to a minor character in the novel, a friend from Austria by the name of Maria. She is a philosophical poetess living in Rome. Maria is a shadowy presence in the novel, modeled on Bernhard's friend Ingeborg Bachmann.[2]

But Maria plays no significant role in the book. The novel is set in motion by the demon mother's death. She is the embodiment of the world Murau was born into, the inescapable fate of his corrupted origins. Even her language, his "leaden" mother tongue, has been weighed down by the burdens of being German. Murau has attempted to escape his Germanness by fleeing into the Romance languages. He envies the "effortlessness and ease and *endlessness* of Italian, which stands in a relationship to German like a child who has grown up completely free in a prosperous and happy household versus one who was repressed and beaten and because of it made cunning [*geschlagen und dadurch verschlagen*] in an impoverished home, the most impoverished." Murau's alienation from his language, of course, calls attention to the more fundamental alienation from himself, his origins, his own identity. But the notion of family, which is so familiar in Bernhard's stock of images, also calls attention to the novel's central image. The metaphor of language as a family home, and especially the idea of a "mother tongue" (*Muttersprache*) strikes near the novel's center of gravity: the death of Murau's mother and the presence of her mangled body throughout the novel.

Her death could mean his emancipation from the mother and all that she stands for; but the nature of her death suggests no victory of the moral order. She perishes not as a result of her reprehensible life but absurdly, in a random car crash, the fault of the truck driver who ran into the car in which she was a passenger. And instead of being liberated, the younger Murau son's captivity is made straiter. He is called home for more than the funeral. He is drawn back to Wolfsegg from his self-imposed exile to become the unwilling patriarch of the Murau clan. There is no escape, insists the novel's plot, from one's own birth. The Austrian who abandons his homeland and language remains an Austrian in spite of his best efforts to transcend the identity.

Though the mother's accidental death suggests no larger moral order at work, her mutilated corpse carries ethical connotations specific to Bernhard's symbolic order. More than any other figure in the family, the mother represents Austria itself. Like the mother, Austria is *verstümmelt*, a favorite Bernhard adjective for Austria that means "mutilated," "maimed," or "mangled":

> The very thought of this mangled and depraved and at bottom irreparably ruined Austria, I thought to myself, I had said to Gambetti just a few days before this almost unendurably tasteless burial, makes me ill, to say nothing of this thoroughly depraved state, Gambetti, whose vulgarity and nastiness are without example not only within Europe but in the whole world; for decades nasty and depraved and dimwitted governments and a people mangled to death beyond recognition by these nasty and depraved and dimwitted governments, I had said to Gambetti, I thought to myself.

When, toward the end of the novel, unreformed old Nazis converge on Wolfsegg for the funeral of the three dead Muraus, Bernhard intends for us to see the maimed soul of modern Austria. Its essence was destroyed in the

Second World War; all that remains is for the living dead to disappear, one by one, until nothing remains of Austria. As the book's title implies, Austria will be *ausgelöscht*, "extinguished."

Ortega y Gasset's famous remark—that man has no nature, only a history—finds a powerful formulation in Bernhard's fiction, and especially in *Auslöschung*. History dissolves into what only appears to be immutable "nature." It takes shape as national guilt, as family identity, and even as the dominant trait of self in the anxiety-ridden protagonist. Naturally Franz-Josef Murau must die too, presumably because he cannot bear the identity that has been thrust upon him. His book closes with the disembodied narrative voice—which emerges only on the first and last pages of the book—reporting on his death, but without divulging its cause. After the funeral Murau's will discloses his plan for Wolfsegg to his two sisters. It is a plan that will obliterate the family and its holdings while at the same time seeking to strike a blow against history. Murau donates the family estate and all its holdings to the Jewish community of Vienna, which is led by his old friend from student days, Rabbi Eisenberg.

Bernhard's moral stance in *Auslöschung* calls to mind the so-called *Vergangenheitsbewältigung* that preoccupies many writers in the contemporary German-speaking world. The word means "mastering the past" and refers to the postwar need to deal with the Nazi era as an ineradicable fact of modern German history and life. Murau's reflections on his family at least seem to draw Bernhard's novel into the circle of contemporary German novelists who attempt to discover and explore the "lessons" of German history.[3] But Thomas Bernhard does not believe in the lessons of history or the possibility of a future. His theme is not historical renewal but its obliteration. The annihilation he envisions rests on an ethic that can fairly be called a *moral anarchism* because his highest value is moral rightness alone.

When history irreversibly transgresses against moral rightness, Bernhard will settle for no atonement except the complete obliteration of the offender, even when it includes his protagonist. Murau's gesture of dissolving the family estate and giving it to the victims of National Socialism remains the impotent gesture of a dead man. It gives the measure of his moral worth, but it also disclaims the possibility of any future community. The symbolic "family" dies with its last scion.

Rather than breaking down mythic structures in order to open the path of reason, Bernhard aggressively asserts a counter-myth of despair, anarchy, and annihilation. Nevertheless, the moral unease that Bernhard's pitiless satire injects into the intellectual life of Germany and Austria must be respected as a thoughtful perspective on the process of *Vergangenheitsbewältigung*, however disheartening it may be.

At least Bernhard does not succumb to the facile temptation of moralizing politics. Politically overcommitted art, both on the right and on the left, forces progressive art, which is committed to the harsher but more humane ethic of insight, into the straits of negation and skepticism.[4] The nay-sayer begins the work of freeing his mind by saying *No!* to the various masks of domination. Bernhard doubts all forms of authority, including putatively utopian literature. As a child of Nazi Austria, as an opponent of authoritarianism in any form Bernhard knows only too well the danger of seeking fulfillment in illusions: the thousand-year Reich, the promise of a rich afterlife, the literary utopias.

NOTES

1. Bernhard does not name the photographer, but presumably Reger means Digne Meller Marcovicz and her photo essay *Martin Heidegger: Photographien* (Frankfurt am Main: Klostermann, 1985).

2. Bachmann died in Rome in 1973, possibly a suicide. Bernhard refers to her ("the most intelligent and most significant poet of our country") in *Der Stimmenimitator* (Frankfurt am Main: Suhrkamp, 1978) 167f.

3. Judith Ryan has studied the complexities of this theme in her *The Uncompleted Past: Postwar German Novels and the Third Reich* (Detroit: Wayne State University Press, 1983).

4. Theodor W. Adorno's critique of Brecht's didactic commitment to communism is the classic statement of how the politics of autonomous art elicits an ultimately more compelling response than doctrinaire didacticism can. Kafka, Beckett, and Picasso are his counterexamples to Brecht. Bernhard would fit easily into his argument. Theodor W. Adorno, "Commitment," *Aesthetics and Politics*, ed. Ronald Taylor (London: Verso, 1980) 177–95.

CHAPTER SIX

Bernhard as Playwright

The last Thomas Bernhard drama to premiere was *Elisabeth II*. The play was published in 1987 and appeared on the stage two years later, at the Schiller-Theater in Berlin in November 1989, nine months after Bernhard's death. The play was vintage Bernhard—hard-bitten, uncompromising, and musical—but Claus Peymann, Bernhard's usual director, did not stage the production; the usual Bernhard stars (Bernhard Minetti, Bruno Ganz, Edith Heerdegen, Paula Wessely) did not participate; and the master himself was dead. The play was a failure with the public and the critics. Somehow the fire had gone out.

The reasons seem clear enough. Bernhard's dramas are not intended to be masterpieces. They are immediate and direct, sensational and spontaneous, tied to time, place, and even to particular actors. The plays are brief spectacles that pierce the heart of a transient mood and then die. When read, Bernhard's works for the stage seem thin and ephemeral in comparison with his prose fiction. They lack the concentrated intellectual energy that he lavished on his novels. Though it does not ring true at all, Bernhard spoke of the theater dismissively, even disparagingly: "The curtain goes up, there's a dungheap on the stage, more and more flies show up, the curtain goes down." In addition, he claimed that his prose works did not produce much income ("press runs of only a few thousand copies, as is the case with unknown beginners"). He referred to his plays, with the attendant nuance of triviality, as moneymakers. And Bernhard did not have a great deal of respect for the theater or for theater people (with certain exceptions; e.g., the actor Bernhard Minetti)—or at least that was his claim.[1] Nevertheless, he wrote eighteen full-length plays and a number of brief dramas between 1967 and 1989, and he had two more unfinished plays on his desk when he died. His works for the stage were highly successful in German theaters during the 1970s and 1980s. For them to be understood properly, two basic features must be considered. The plays should be seen in the light of performance, first of all, but also in the context of their then contemporary setting.

Bernhard's musical verbal style—always stripped of punctuation and printed on the page with the appearance of verse—is a difficult medium that calls for a special declamatory performance. Only the finest actors, those trained in classical theater, can make Bernhard's theater work. "In my opinion drama is primarily a matter of language," says Bernhard; "of course there is also the theater of somersaults, where people flipflop around, constantly running in and out of doors, deciding fates every few minutes. . . . My dramas are different. You have to listen. My drama evolves slowly, out of the language itself, and by that I do not mean my personal experience but my idea of dramatic literature."[2] Minetti is the master of Bernhardian language. But in the hands of lesser actors, even actors who work well in the conventional stage idiom, Bernhard's plays seem bloodless and dull. *Einfach kompliziert* (Simply Complicated, 1986), to name only one of many possible examples, was a monologue written with Minetti in mind. And in fact Minetti's performance of the piece was mesmerizing. Still, the fascination does not carry over into reading. The play becomes flat, even boring, because the music has evaporated and because Minetti's strong stage presence is missing.

Die Jagdgesellschaft (1974; translated as *The Hunting Party*, 1980) is another example of the relative fragility of Bernhard's theater writing. It was the first of Bernhard's plays to be performed at Vienna's venerable Burgtheater. The play had been written, according to Bernhard, with Bruno Ganz and Paula Wessely in mind. Unfortunately, the Burgtheater ensemble objected to outsiders performing lead roles in the play. Because he was bound by contract, Bernhard reluctantly (to say the least) let the Burgtheater cast the play. In Bernhard's opinion, and in the critics' opinions, the play was a flop, though by all accounts the Burgtheater is one of the finest theaters in the German-speaking world.

Bernhard considered himself an actor's dramatist. As he said on more than one occasion, he wrote plays intending to offer his actors the opportunity to unfold their talents. In fact, he often wrote for specific actors, and above all for Bernhard Minetti. *Minetti: Porträt des Künstlers als alter Mann* (Minetti: Portrait of the Artist as an Old Man, 1976) is unabashedly a vehicle for the talent of Bernhard's favorite actor. *Ritter, Dene, Voss* (1984; translated as *Ritter, Dene, Voss*, 1990) was written and named for actors in Claus Peymann's troupe: Gert Voss, Kirsten Dene, Ilse Ritter. Works so closely tied to specific actors and troupes easily droop and fade when performed by other actors in places not attuned to the intellectual fashion of following Bernhard, the celebrity playwright, and Peymann, the celebrity director.

But there is yet another element of performance that must be considered: that of Bernhard himself. I suggested that one reason for the failure of *Elisabeth II* in Berlin was its author's death. In a wider sense than acting on the stage, Bernhard contributed to the "performance" of his works. Even before the 1970 premiere of his first play, *Ein Fest für Boris* (translated as *A Party for Boris*, 1990), he had a reputation for cantankerous behavior and a scorched-earth tactics in satirical writing. His public was eager to see what powerful figure he would insult next, what enraged outcry he would elicit, who would try to sue him, and how he would respond. To put it baldly, Bernhard's plays were also media events.[3] In 1972, for example, *Der Ignorant und der Wahnsinnige* (The Ignoramus and the Madman) premiered at the Salzburg Festival. Bernhard insisted that for symbolic effect the house lights should go out at the end of the play, fire exit signs included. The fire marshal refused; the festival authorities refused; Bernhard insisted; and the whole incident became histrionically inflated with articles, heated exchanges, and telegrams.

Die Berühmten (The Big Names) caused a similar flap in 1975. The Salzburg Festival commissioned Bernhard to write a play for its 1976 season. But when festival officials learned that Bernhard was writing a play that lampooned the big names associated with the Salzburg Festival, they reneged. The usual spate of public and private letters, angry accusations and newspaper editorials ensued. Observers thought that Bernhard's association with the Salzburg Festival had surely come to an end. Astonishingly, he was again invited to write for the festival in 1981 (*Am Ziel* [The Goal Attained]) and in 1984. In *Der Theatermacher* (1984; *Histrionics*, 1990) Bernhard satirized himself and the fire exit episode of 1972.

But theater and art as such also come under attack. According to Bruscon, the protagonist of *Histrionics*, human beings are liars and hypocrites, "and nowhere else in this humanity / is the falseness greater and more fascinating / than in the theater." Bruscon, who is an actor, "says that theater is an absurdity":

>
> but if we are honest
> we can't put on a show
> nor can we if we are honest
> write a stage play
> or act in a stage play
> if we are honest

> we can't do anything anymore
> except kill ourselves
> but since we don't kill ourselves
> because we don't want to kill ourselves
> at least not up to now and not so far
> so since we have not up to now and not so far killed ourselves
> we keep giving the theater another try[.]

Now, Bruscon's attitude is not exactly in the spirit of the Salzburg Festival tradition. It is ironic that Bernhard was ever invited to write plays for the festival at all. Given the undisguised aesthetic nihilism of Bernhard's writing, the Salzburg Festival seems an unlikely setting for his attack on the premises of the Western theatrical tradition.

The festival was established in 1920 by dramatist Hugo von Hofmannsthal, composer Richard Strauss, and stage director Max Reinhardt as a symbol of Austrian national identity and spiritual unity. The gradual disintegration and final collapse of the Habsburg empire after World War I created a vacuum in the Austrian sense of national identity. Robbed of a continuous political history, intellectuals sought to renew for Austria its historical legitimation and self-definition by way of the artistic tradition. Hofmannsthal, Strauss, and Reinhardt specifically were attempting to reconnect a war-battered Austria with itself through art.[4] Cultural unity was to compensate for military defeat and political dissolution.

Music and theater lent themselves well to the task of refashioning Austrian identity because cultural ideals seemed fixed beyond the contingencies of history: the Catholic tradition of Austrian baroque that Hofmannsthal worked to renew in his dramas and libretti; the music of Mozart and Beethoven, and the new compositions of Strauss; the stagecraft of Vienna's brilliant director Max Reinhardt employed to renew the classics. In the high-flown rhetoric of Richard Strauss, the festival was to be "a symbol filled with the light of truth and the reflected glory of our culture. All Europe shall know that our future lies in art. . . . In times during which the possessions of the spirit are rarer than material goods and during which egoism, envy, hate and mistrust appear to rule, he who supports our proposition will have done something good and helped to reestablish brotherly love and human kindness."[5] It is instructive to compare Strauss's post–World War I pathos with Bernhard's post–World War II bathos:

> The spirit of Salzburg therefore is throughout the year the *perverted* spirit ["*Un*geist"] of Catholicism and National Socialism, and the rest is

a lie. In the summertime under the name of the Salzburg Festival, the city hypocritically affects a pose of universality, and the medium of so-called international art is only a means of disguising the perversity of its perverted spirit, just like all the summers here are fakery, hypocrisy, attempts at setting to music and playing away [the perversity] of a city and its residents who during the summers misuse so-called Great Art for vulgar ends of commerce, the Festivals are put on in order to cover up the mire of the city.

His words here could serve as a gloss on the plays he wrote for the Salzburg Festival.[6] Of them the most characteristic is probably his comedy entitled *Die Macht der Gewohnheit* (1974; *The Force of Habit*, 1976). It, too, satirizes the Salzburg Festival, but with more finesse than *Die Berühmten*. Bernhard repackages the festival as a small and shabby family circus. As always the idea of family echoes the idea of nation. At its center is Caribaldi (originally played by Minetti), the paterfamilias and circus director, who for twenty-two years has been trying to extract a perfect performance of Schubert's *Trout Quintet* from his inept circus performers. They, the performers, have neither talent nor interest. Even Caribaldi's hopes have faded, yet the ill-tempered tyrant continues to enforce a regimen of daily rehearsals on the unwilling quintet. Caribaldi speaks here to his juggler:

>   The truth is
> I do not love the cello
> It tortures me
> but it has to be played
> my granddaughter does not love the viola
> but it has to be played
> the clown does not love the bass violin
> but it has to be played
> the lion tamer does not love the piano
> but it has to be played
> And you do not love the violin
> We do not want life
> but it has to be lived
> We hate the Trout Quintet
> but it has to be played[.]

In this play, which was composed especially for the festival, Bernhard is speaking primarily to the Salzburg Festival audience, to its participants, and to the festival authorities. What has kept the music alive all these years in Salzburg, he asserts, is only the force of habit. The grand festival is at bottom a small-time family circus undone by ineptitude and chaos. Thus *The Force of Habit* embodies one of Bernhard's two basic themes in drama: the failure of art to redeem the individual, the nation, the family, or anything else. Art, like life, is a burden borne unwillingly.

The other fundamental theme is historical. Bernhard confronts the problem of the Nazi past with great directness, especially in *Vor dem Ruhestand* (1979; *Eve of Retirement*, 1982) and *Heldenplatz* (1988). Both plays were directed by Claus Peymann, and they excited a great deal of controversy. Bernhard favored the ensemble of the avant-garde director, who staged nearly all the Bernhard premieres. Along with other self-willed directors of the period (e.g., George Tabori, Peter Stein, Peter Zadek), Peymann bucked the prevailing taste of West German theater in the 1970s for conservative productions of the classics on the one hand, and for politically committed Brechtian theater on the other. His productions emphasized directorial imagination and interpretation. Bernhard's plays, with minimal stage directions and a tendency toward the outrageous and offensive, suited his talents well.

Bernhard wrote *Eve of Retirement* for Peymann in 1979, at a time when West Germany was in the grip of a conservative wave of reaction to terrorist acts by the Red Army Faction and the Baader-Meinhof gang. Peymann, who at that time was the artistic director of the Staatstheater in Stuttgart (capital of Baden-Württemberg), had long been criticized by the conservative politicians of the Christian Democratic Union. His theater, like most German theaters, was heavily subsidized by the state, and its leading politicians wondered if its money was being well spent by the avant-garde director. Not the least of his critics was the Minister President of Baden-Württemberg, the outspoken law-and-order conservative Hans Karl Filbinger.

Apart from their general dislike of his theater, a particular incident irritated the state authorities. In 1977 Peymann was approached by the mother of convicted terrorist Gudrun Ennslin. She asked the theater director to solicit contributions on behalf of her daughter who, while imprisoned in a maximum security facility near Stuttgart, needed some expensive dental work. Peymann posted a notice on the Staatstheater bulletin board, which soon caused an uproar in the papers and in conservative political circles. Some branded Peymann a sympathizer with the terrorist cause, while others (notably Stuttgart mayor Rommel) supported his right to solicit funds for anyone he wanted as long as it was legal. Minister President Filbinger and his allies eventually forced Peymann to resign as artistic director of the Württembergisches Staatstheater.

But Peymann's main detractors soon found themselves in an awkward position. In July of 1978 it was discovered that Minister President Filbinger, whose name was being passed around the Christian Democratic Union as a potential presidential candidate for the whole of West Germany, had long concealed his sordid activities as a naval judge during and after the Second World War. At issue were the numerous death sentences he handed down as a zealous agent of Nazi justice, including capital sentences for trivial offenses. In a pattern that the Austrian presidential candidate Kurt Waldheim would repeat in the 1980s, Filbinger at first lied stubbornly about ever having given out death sentences at all. When the truth became incontrovertible, Filbinger—incredibly—tried to trivialize their importance. After vigorous persuasion by his embarrassed colleagues in the Christian Democratic Union, Filbinger finally resigned his post and retired from politics.

The Filbinger affair unfolded and was completed before Peymann's resignation as artistic director in Stuttgart took effect. As his swan song he had planned to stage Rolf Hochhuth's docudrama *Die Juristen* (The Lawyers), which was based on the Filbinger affair. But when Hochhuth failed to meet the deadline, Peymann staged Bernhard's *Eve of Retirement* instead (June 1979). While Bernhard's drama is not directly based on the Filbinger case, it is best understood as a response to the controversy that affair aroused and the public issues that it raised.

The play's subtitle, "A Comedy of the German Soul," gives a good indication of what Bernhard was attempting, even if his "comedy" is not funny. As always Bernhard is interested in plumbing the inner realm of outward events, which means in *Eve of Retirement* an unblinking exploration of German repression of the past. Filbinger represented for Bernhard, and many others, a larger German failure to reckon adequately with the meaning of National Socialism. Particularly galling, obviously, was the rise of the Nazi hanging judge to a place of wealth, prestige, and public trust in a democratic country that had putatively settled with its past. Filbinger served as a symbol for the pernicious continuity between past and present in Germany, and at a time when state policy on terrorism had brought to a seeming impasse the conflict between the government (represented in the authoritarian person of Filbinger himself) and individual rights. Bernhard responded with a glimpse into the family life of a Filbinger-like German chief justice on the eve of his retirement from the bench.

The domestic scenes of his family life stand for the private, taboo, repressed past of a whole nation, the "German soul" of Bernhard's subtitle. On the seventh of every October, Justice Rudolf Höller and his two sisters, Vera and Clara, have for decades secretly celebrated the birthday of SS chief Heinrich Himmler. Höller had served as a concentration camp commandant under Himmler during the war, and remembers those days with warm nostalgia. Champagne, a fine meal set to strains of Mozart and Beethoven, and a ramble through the family photo album begin an evening that is peppered with Höller's demented tirades against Jewry, Americans, and democracy.

Once the Höllers have finished wallowing in memories of National Socialism, the chief justice and his sister Vera top off the evening by retiring to bed for their annual session of incestuous lovemaking. The other sister, Clara, belongs to the ranks of Bernhard's oppressed and powerless female characters. She does not share the obscene pleasures of her brother and sister. Clara sympathizes with democracy and socialism, but she cannot defend herself against Rudolf and Vera. Clara is an invalid, bound to a wheelchair as a result of an American bombing mission during the war. The voice of liberal reason in "the Höller family" is unable to assert its rights.

Eve of Retirement succeeds as satire because it ruthlessly probes the open wounds of German consciousness and historical identity. Not only do its characters speak the unspeakable, but they do so in a blood-chilling matter-of-fact way that lends to the play its eerie, even frightening nimbus of authenticity. "Who would have thought it Vera," says Rudolf as he cheerfully ponders his life since the war:

> Times change so much
> First ten years of hiding in a miserable cellar
> hidden by you and Clara
> then all of a sudden this change for the better
> I don't have a bad conscience
> Now and again things look dark that is still true today
> but I don't have a bad conscience
> I should be the last one to have a bad conscience
> I only did my duty
> and I spared no effort
> I went to work and got more done
> than anyone could have demanded
> I spared no effort
> I find nothing to fault myself for[.]

Höller's clean conscience, which is Bernhard's satirical image of German national consciousness, is harrowing. Still, Bernhard does not become a political playwright with *Eve of Retirement*. He offers no positive vision of critical reason, which he embodies in the sad and permanently disabled Clara.

The vitriolic rage that Bernhard pours into his play is not that of a liberal intellectual committed to a politics based on the application of critical reason. Instead, Bernhard's views are those of a *moral anarchist*. Intellectual liberals—especially those associated with the influential Hamburg weekly journal of opinion *Die Zeit*—followed Bernhard closely and sympathetically for the most part, and Bernhard frequently published in their pages. They shared his critically incisive views on Germany's past (and Austria's), and they encouraged the discussion that his irreverent books and plays generated. But in spite of the intellectual company he kept, Bernhard himself remained a moral anarchist: "anarchical" in the sense that his views represent a moral revolt against the natural tendency to forgive and forget with the passage of time. "I always take up the subject of those dreadful times," writes Bernhard of the Nazi era, "but people just shake their heads. In me these terrible experiences are just as present as if they had been only yesterday." Bernhard refuses to accept the passage of time and its process of forgetting (and healing) because it is ethically unacceptable. His revolt has nothing to do with a systematic platform of ideas and values that could be translated into a political agenda. Bernhard's ethical standards stem from an internal moral absolute that is personal and hopelessly pessimistic, one that knows no compromise, no forgiveness, and no political praxis outside of literature.

Nevertheless, certain of Bernhard's works have a political, social, and historical dimension with implications for political life, as the editors of *Die Zeit* plainly understood. Apart from *Eve of Retirement* the most important of them is his final published drama, *Heldenplatz*, written for the Burgtheater, which in 1987 had come under the leadership of Claus Peymann. Bernhard wrote the play for a double occasion. The year 1988 marked not only the hundredth anniversary of Vienna's Burgtheater; it was also the fiftieth anniversary of Hitler's triumphant arrival in Vienna. On 15 March 1938 Hitler spoke before throngs of Austrians jubilant over their country's annexation to the prosperous Third Reich. Vienna's Heldenplatz, which is only a short walk down the Ringstrasse from the Burgtheater, was the scene of Hitler's speech.

In *Heldenplatz* Bernhard grinds salt in the open wound of Austrian antisemitism. "The situation is much worse now than fifty years ago" is a refrain that recurs throughout the drama with awful insistence. The play concentrates on a group of Austrian Jews—in an apartment near the Heldenplatz and the Volksgarten, within sight of the Burgtheater—who have gathered in March of 1988 for the funeral of Professor Josef Schuster. Five decades earlier the Nazis had driven the philosopher Schuster into English exile because he was a Jew, but after the war, now a famous Oxford professor, he was coaxed back to his native Vienna. Ultimately, however, he found Austria intolerable, and committed suicide shortly before he had planned to return permanently with his wife to England.

His wife is the key to Bernhard's less-than-subtle theme. Frau Schuster suffers acutely from the inability to forget. In Vienna she still hears the raving masses of 1938 from the nearby Heldenplatz. In this context Bernhard's personal view about the Third Reich bears repeating once more. "In me," he says, the terrible experiences of the Nazi era "are just as present as if they had been only yesterday." Frau Schuster embodies his rejection of time. Even electrotherapy at Steinhof, the local mental institution, has not obliterated her vivid memories of persecution and dehumanization. From Bernhard's perspective her madness is a form of moral sanity.

Basically, the death and funeral that serve as the drama's focal point represent the end of Austria. Schuster is not so much an Austrian *Jew* as an *Austrian* Jew. The persecution of Austrians by Austrians signals the inward collapse of whatever spirit once made the concept of Austria cohere—an empire of multiple nationalities and races—into a cohesive whole. The Austrian in Schuster makes life elsewhere an impossibility, and Austria itself makes life in his homeland an impossibility. The conflict is strongly reminiscent of the impasse experienced by the essayist Jean Améry, which he writes about in his penetrating memoir *At the Mind's Limits* (1966). Bernhard may or may not have had the Austrian émigré philosopher in mind when he invented Schuster. Even if he did not, the parallels are too revealing to pass over without discussion.

Améry is an anagram of Maier, the name he was born with in Vienna in 1912. Hans Maier's father was an Austrian patriot, a Jewish soldier who died fighting for Emperor Franz Joseph in World War I. His mother was a German Austrian. Hans Maier never thought much about his Jewishness until the Nuremberg Laws of 1935 cut through the middle of his identity. His Jewish blood suddenly transformed him into an alien in his own homeland, whether he liked it or not. With the incorporation of Austria into Nazi Germany, Maier fled to Belgium, where he became a member of the underground resistance. He was captured in 1943, tortured by the Gestapo, and eventually interned in a series of concentration camps, including Auschwitz. But Maier survived, and then tried to shape a new identity for himself in Belgium as Jean Améry—philosopher, journalist, photographer.

During the 1970s Améry became a well-known figure in German and Austrian intellectual life. Without surrendering to the sentimentalities of the holocaust industry that was beginning to flourish, he expressed his resentments and hatred of what the Germans and Austrians had done to him with precise insight. It is not without relevance that Améry wrote approvingly of Bernhard's memoir *The Cause* and his novel *Correction*.[7] But what seems most important is the attitude of permanent resentment that the two writers share. Like Bernhard, Améry refuses to let bygones be bygones. Neither writer believes that true progress has been made in the postwar era. Despite the best efforts of right-thinking Germans and others, writes Améry with sober pessimism, "Hitler's Reich will, for the time being, continue to be regarded as an operational accident of history." He continues:

> Finally, however, it will be purely and simply history, no better and no worse than dramatic historical epochs just happen to be, bloodstained perhaps, but after all also a Reich that had its everyday family life. . . . The former general staff officer Prince Ferdinand von der Leyen writes, " . . . from one of our detachments came even more horrible news. SS units had broken into the houses there and from the upper floors they had thrown children, who were still unable to walk, through the windows onto the pavement." But such murder of millions as this, carried out by a highly civilized people, with organizational dependability and almost scientific precision, will be lumped with the bloody expulsion of the Armenians by the Turks or with the shameful acts of the colonial French: as regrettable, but in no way unique. Everything will be submerged in a "Century of Barbarism." *We*, the victims, will appear as the truly incorrigible, irreconcilable ones, as the antihistorical reactionaries in the exact sense of the word, and in the end it will seem like a technical mishap that some of us survived.[8]

Bernhard's most horrific inventions pale by comparison with Prince von der Leyen's report. But comparison also suggests a possible spiritual source for Bernhard's teratology of the German soul. Like Jean Améry, Bernhard seems incorrigible in his animus against Austria, irreconcilable to history and therefore "antihistorical" in his refusal to let the passage of time do its work of healing. *Heldenplatz*, however rude and mean-spirited it may seem, forces a moral confrontation between past and present—and all the more so in Vienna during the amnesiac presidency of Kurt Waldheim.

There is one other significant link between Améry and Bernhard. It is the resemblance between Améry and Josef Schuster (and Franz-Josef Murau of *Auslöschung*). Améry never really freed himself of his Austrian identity. He changed his name and his country, but he continued to write in his native language, the language of the oppressors; like it or not, his cultural and intellectual background remained Austrian-German, even though he was morally unable to identify with the nation that had driven him into exile, murdered his kind, and robbed the survivors of the right to feel at home in their own past, in their own language, and in their own culture. In 1978 Améry returned to Austria, and in fact to Bernhard's hometown of Salzburg, evidently for the express purpose of hanging himself. He did not explain his reasons for taking his own life, yet it is difficult not to connect his suicide with the resentments, losses, and hatred that he expresses in *At the Mind's Limits*.

Schuster's leap from his apartment window in *Heldenplatz* (and Frau Schuster's sudden death at the end of the play) can be interpreted from the perspective of Améry's suicide. Schuster was not at home in England so he came back to his native Austria, but he discovered that it could no longer be his home. The past, symbolized as a home with a view of the notorious Heldenplatz, was too much for both husband and wife. One actively takes his own life, and the other simply collapses under the strain of life among the people who had once tried to destroy her, her family, and her entire race.

Understandably, Austrian Jews, a tiny minority in present-day Austria, did not greet Bernhard's play with enthusiasm. Some objected to the apparently self-righteous Thomas Bernhard, a non-Jew, arrogating to himself the right to speak out against Austria in their interest. To make matters worse, Kurt Waldheim's sordid campaign for the presidency of Austria and his subsequent election in 1986 left a residue of anti-Jewish sentiment among some Austrians. The last thing an Austrian Jew needed was a wildly accusatory drama by Thomas Bernhard stirring up anti-semitic feelings. Of course it would be a mistake to suppose that Bernhard intended to speak on behalf of the Jewish community. No doubt he identified to a certain extent with Austrian Jewry; their fate belongs to his basic idea of the way Austria deals with its children. But the more compelling reason for his portrayal of Jews in contemporary Austria must have been his anarchic morality. Always intransigent in his ethics, always eager to make himself known at any cost, Bernhard was willing to offend anyone—and everyone—in the interest of a bitter moral truth.

Bernhard's theater was total theater, especially in Austria. It transcended the stage and spilled over into the streets. Hardly a soul, it seemed, was left uninvolved in the histrionic controversy around *Heldenplatz*. As one of the characters in the play puts it:

> What remains to this poor disenfranchised people
> is nothing but the theater
> Austria itself is nothing but a stage
> on which everything is ruined squandered and wasted.

Trouble began early, when it was announced that Bernhard was working in secret on an offering for the Burgtheater jubilee. Objections were raised at the choice of Bernhard to write for the occasion at all, but also against Claus Peymann, a West German, dominating Austria's most historically important theater. Originally the play was scheduled for an October 1988 debut. But when excerpts appeared in the press, a public scandal erupted. Some of the Burgtheater ensemble refused to participate in Bernhard's drama, which resulted in the premiere being postponed until November.

The public furor around the production was astonishing.[9] Politicians fulminated against Bernhard's anti-Austrian play and against the "waste" of public funds on his works. Kurt Waldheim denounced the play as "a vulgar insult to the Austrian people." There were demonstrations in the streets against Bernhard and his play. His supporters, too, staged demonstrations of their own against the opponents and in support of the play. Heated exchanges occurred in newspapers, coffee houses, and living rooms all over Austria. Poison pen letters and even death threats were sent to both Bernhard and Peymann. But the play went on.

Heldenplatz was the last Bernhard play to appear on the Austrian stage. In February of 1989 Bernhard died of Boek's disease (sarcoidosis) but not without fomenting a posthumous scandal. When his will became public, it was learned that Bernhard had made a strange entailment: none of his books is to be published in Austria and none of his plays is to be staged there for the duration of his copyright, seventy years. As the news of his will spread in Austria, there was an immediate run on his works in bookstores.

NOTES

1. Kurt Hofmann, ed., *Aus Gesprächen mit Thomas Bernhard* (Vienna: Löcker, 1988) 78–79.

2. Quoted in Jens Dittmar, ed., *Thomas Bernhard Werkgeschichte*, 2d rev. ed. (Frankfurt am Main: Suhrkamp, 1990) 231.

3. Because they were difficult to read and had a smaller following, his novels did not lend themselves to the same media excitement as his plays. The notable exception was *Cutting Timber*, which generated the kind of circus that was common for the plays.

4. Michael P. Steinberg has written an illuminating history of the festival: *The Meaning of the Salzburg Festival: Austria as Theater and Ideology 1890–1938* (Ithaca: Cornell University Press, 1990).

5. Walter Pankofsky, *Richard Strauss: Partitur eines Lebens* (Munich: Piper, 1965) 235.

6. *Der Ignorant und der Wahnsinnige*, Salzburg Festival, 29 July 1972; *Die Macht der Gewohnheit*, Salzburg Festival, 27 July 1974; *Die Berühmten*, Vienna, Theater an der Wien, 8 June 1976; *Am Ziel*, a co-production of the Salzburg Festival (18 Aug. 1981) and the Bochum Schauspielhaus (22 Oct. 1981); *Der Theatermacher*, a co-production of the Salzburg Festival (17 Aug. 1985) and the Bochum Schauspielhaus (21 Sept. 1985); *Ritter, Dene, Voss*, a co-production of the Salzburg Festival (18 Aug. 1986) and the Burgtheater in Vienna (4 Sept. 1986).

7. Jean Améry, "Morbus Austriacus," *Merkur* 30 (1976): 91–96.

8. Jean Améry, *At the Mind's Limits: Contemplations by a Survivor on Auschwitz and Its Realities*, trans. Sidney Rosenfeld and Stella P. Rosenfeld (New York: Schocken, 1990) 79–80.

9. Jens Dittmar offers a representative selection of the responses in his indispensable *Thomas Bernhard Werkgeschichte* 330–37.

BIBLIOGRAPHY

Works by Thomas Bernhard

BOOKS

Auf der Erde und in der Hölle: Gedichte. Salzburg: Otto Müller, 1957.
In hora mortis. Salzburg: Otto Müller, 1958.
Unter dem Eisen des Mondes: Gedichte. Cologne, Berlin: Kiepenheuer & Witsch, 1958.
die rosen der einöde: fünf sätze für ballett, stimmen, und orchester. Frankfurt am Main: Fischer, 1959.
Frost. Frankfurt am Main: Insel, 1963. Excerpt translated by Helene Scher in *Postwar German Culture*. New York: Dutton, 1974. 238–42.
Amras. Frankfurt am Main: Insel, 1964.
Prosa. Frankfurt am Main: Suhrkamp, 1967.
Verstörung. Frankfurt am Main: Insel, 1967. Trans. by Richard and Clara Winston as *Gargoyles*. New York: Knopf, 1970.
Ungenach: Erzählung. Frankfurt am Main: Suhrkamp, 1968.
An der Baumgrenze: Erzählungen. Salzburg: Residenz, 1969. Trans. by Sophie Wilkins as "At the Timberline" in *Anthology of Modern Austrian Literature*. Ed. Adolf Opel. Atlantic Heights, NJ: Humanities Press, 1981. 187–91.
Ereignisse. Berlin: Literarisches Kolloquium, 1969.
Watten: Ein Nachlaß. Frankfurt am Main: Suhrkamp, 1969.
Das Kalkwerk. Frankfurt am Main: Suhrkamp, 1970. Trans. by Sophie Wilkins as *The Lime Works*. New York: Knopf, 1973.
Der Italiener. Salzburg: Residenz, 1971.
Midland in Stilfs: Drei Erzählungen. Frankfurt am Main: Suhrkamp, 1971.
Gehen. Frankfurt am Main: Suhrkamp, 1971.
Der Kulterer: Eine Filmgeschichte. Salzburg: Residenz, 1974.
Die Ursache: Eine Andeutung. Salzburg: Residenz, 1975. Trans. by David McLintock as "An Indication of the Cause" in *Gathering Evidence: A Memoir*. New York: Knopf, 1985. 75–141.
Korrektur. Frankfurt am Main: Suhrkamp, 1975. Trans. by Sophie Wilkins as *Correction*. New York: Knopf, 1979.
Der Wetterfleck: Erzählungen. Stuttgart: Reclam, 1976.

Der Keller: Eine Entziehung. Salzburg: Residenz, 1976. Trans. by David McLintock as "The Cellar: An Escape" in *Gathering Evidence: A Memoir.* New York: Knopf, 1985. 142–213.
Der Atem: Eine Entscheidung. Salzburg: Residenz, 1978. Trans. by David McLintock as "Breath: A Decision" in *Gathering Evidence: A Memoir.* New York: Knopf, 1985. 215–275.
Ja. Frankfurt am Main: Suhrkamp, 1978.
Der Stimmenimitator. Frankfurt am Main: Suhrkamp, 1978.
Die Erzählungen. Frankfurt am Main: Suhrkamp, 1979.
Die Billigesser. Frankfurt am Main: Suhrkamp, 1980. Trans. by Ewald Osers as *The Cheap-Eaters.* London: Quartet, 1990.
Die Kälte: Eine Isolation. Salzburg: Residenz, 1981. Trans. by David McLintock as "In the Cold" in *Gathering Evidence: A Memoir.* New York: Knopf, 1985. 277–340.
Ave Vergil. Frankfurt am Main: Suhrkamp, 1981.
Wittgensteins Neffe: Eine Freundschaft. Frankfurt am Main: Suhrkamp, 1982. Trans. by David McLintock as *Wittgenstein's Nephew: A Friendship.* New York: Knopf, 1989.
Ein Kind (Salzburg: Residenz, 1982). Trans. by David McLintock as "A Child" in *Gathering Evidence: A Memoir* New York: Knopf, 1985.
Beton. Frankfurt am Main: Suhrkamp, 1982. Trans. by David McLintock as *Concrete.* New York: Knopf, 1984.
Der Untergeher. Frankfurt am Main: Suhrkamp, 1983.
Holzfällen: Eine Erregung. Frankfurt am Main: Suhrkamp, 1984. Trans. by Ewald Osers as *Cutting Timber.* London: Quartet, 1985. Trans. by David McLintock as *Woodcutters.* New York: Knopf, 1987.
Alte Meister: Komödie. Frankfurt am Main: Suhrkamp, 1985. Trans. by Ewald Osers as *Old Masters.* London: Quartet, 1989.
Auslöschung: Ein Zerfall. Frankfurt am Main: Suhrkamp, 1986.
Stücke, 4 vols. Frankfurt am Main: Suhrkamp, 1988.
Die Irren/Die Häftlinge. Frankfurt am Main: Insel, 1988. Private printing, Klagenfurt: Kleinmayr, 1962.
In der Höhe: Rettungsversuch, Unsinn. Salzburg: Residenz, 1989.

PLAYS

Ein Fest für Boris. (Premiered in Hamburg at the Deutsches Schauspielhaus 29 June 1970.) Frankfurt am Main: Suhrkamp, 1970. Trans. by Peter Jansen and Kenneth Northcott as "Party for Boris" in *Histrionics: Three Plays.* Chicago: University of Chicago Press, 1990. 1–71.
Der Ignorant und der Wahnsinnige. (Premiered at the Salzburg Festival, 29 July 1972.) Frankfurt am Main: Suhrkamp, 1972.

BIBLIOGRAPHY

Die Jagdgesellschaft. (Premiered in Vienna at the Burgtheater, 4 May 1974.) Frankfurt am Main: Suhrkamp, 1974. Trans. by Gitta Honegger as *The Hunting Party. Performing Arts Journal* 5 (1980): 101–31.

Die Macht der Gewohnheit: Komödie. (Premiered at the Salzburg Festival, 27 July 1974.) Frankfurt am Main: Suhrkamp, 1974. Trans. by Neville and Stephen Plaice as *The Force of Habit: A Comedy.* London: Heinemann, 1976.

Der Präsident. (Premiered in Vienna at the Burgtheater, 17 May 1975.) Frankfurt am Main: Suhrkamp, 1975. Trans. by Gitta Honegger in *"The President" and "Eve of Retirement."* New York: Performing Arts Publications, 1982. 17–114.

Die Berühmten. (Premiered in Vienna at the Theater an der Wien, 8 June 1976.) Frankfurt am Main: Suhrkamp, 1976.

Minetti: Porträt des Künstlers als alter Mann. (Premiered in Stuttgart at the Staatstheater, 1 Sept. 1976.) Frankfurt am Main: Suhrkamp, 1976.

Immanuel Kant. (Premiered in Stuttgart at the Staatstheater, 15 April 1978.) Frankfurt am Main: Suhrkamp, 1978.

Vor dem Ruhestand: Eine Komödie von deutscher Seele. (Premiered in Stuttgart at the Staatstheater, 29 June 1979.) Frankfurt am Main: Suhrkamp, 1979. Trans. by Gitta Honegger in *"The President" and "The Eve of Retirement".* New York: Performing Arts Publications, 1982. 115–208.

Der Weltverbesserer. (Premiered in Bochum at the Schauspielhaus, 6 Sept. 1980.) Frankfurt am Main: Suhrkamp, 1979.

Am Ziel. (Premiered as a co-production of the Salzburg Festival, 18 Aug. 1981, and the Bochum Schauspielhaus, 22 Oct. 1981.) Frankfurt am Main: Suhrkamp, 1981.

Der deutsche Mittagstisch: Dramolette. (Premiered in Bochum at the Schauspielhaus, 7 Nov. 1981.) Frankfurt am Main: Suhrkamp, 1988. Trans. by Gitta Honegger as "The German Lunch Table" in *Performing Arts Journal* 6 (1981/82): 26ff.

Über allen Gipfeln ist Ruh. (Premiered in Ludwigsburg at the Castle Festival on 25 June 1982, and in Bochum at the Schauspielhaus, 1 Oct. 1982.) Frankfurt am Main: Suhrkamp, 1981.

Der Schein trügt. (Premiered in Bochum at the Schauspielhaus, 21 Jan. 1984.) Frankfurt am Main: Suhrkamp, 1983. Trans. by Gitta Honegger as "Appearances Are Deceiving" in *Theater* 15 (1983): 13–51.

Der Theatermacher. (Premiered as a co-production of the Salzburg Festival, 17 Aug. 1985, and the Bochum Schauspielhaus, 21 Sept. 1985.) Frankfurt am Main: Suhrkamp, 1984. Trans. by Jansen and Northcott as "Histrionics," in *Histrionics: Three Plays.* Chicago: University of Chicago Press, 1990. 179–282.

Ritter, Dene, Voss. (Premiered at the Salzburg Festival, 18 Aug. 1986.) Frankfurt am Main: Suhrkamp, 1984. Trans. by Jansen and Northcott as "Ritter, Dene, Voss" in *Histrionics: Three Plays.* Chicago: University of Chicago Press, 1990. 73–178.

Einfach kompliziert. (Premiered in West Berlin at the Schiller-Theater, 28 Feb. 1986.) Frankfurt am Main: Suhrkamp, 1986.
Elisabeth II. (Premiered in Berlin at the Schiller-Theater, 5 Nov. 1989.) Frankfurt am Main: Suhrkamp, 1987.
Heldenplatz. (Premiered in Vienna at the Burgtheater, 4 Nov. 1988.) Frankfurt am Main: Suhrkamp, 1988.
Claus Peymann kauft sich eine Hose und geht mit mir essen: Drei Dramolette. Frankfurt am Main: Suhrkamp, 1990.

OTHER

"Großer, unbegreiflicher Hunger." *Stimmen der Gegenwart 1954.* Ed. Hans Weigel. Vienna: Albrecht Dürer, 1954. 138–43.
"Der Schweinehüter." *Stimmen der Gegenwart 1956.* Vienna and Munich: Herold, 1956. 158–79.
"Ein Frühling." *Spektrum des Geistes 1964: Literaturkalender.* Ebenhausen bei München: Hatfrid Voss, [1963]. 36.
"Der Italiener." *Insel-Almanach auf das Jahr 1965.* Frankfurt am Main: Insel, 1964.
"Mit der Klarheit nimmt die Kälte zu." *Jahresring 65/66.* Stuttgart: DVA, 1965. 243–45.
"Nie und mit nichts fertig werden." *Deutsche Akademie für Sprache und Dichtung, Jahrbuch 1970.* Heidelberg and Darmstadt: Schneider, 1971. 83–84.

PERIODICAL PUBLICATIONS:

"Ein Zeugenaussage." *Wort in der Zeit* 10 (1964): 38–43.
"Ein junger Schriftsteller." *Wort in der Zeit* 11 (1965): 56–59.
"Politische Morgenandacht." *Wort in der Zeit* 12 (1966): 11–13.
"Unsterblichkeit ist unmöglich: Landschaft der Kindheit." *Neues Forum* 169/170 (1968): 95–97.
"Die Wahrheit und dem Tod auf der Spur: Zwei Reden." *Neues Forum* 173 (1968): 347–49.
"Ein Fest für Boris." *Theater heute* 11 (Jan. 1970): 39–47.
"Der Berg," *Literatur und Kritik* 46 (1970): 330–52.
"Vor der Akademie." *Frankfurter Allgemeine Zeitung,* 19 Oct. 1970: 22.
"Als Verwalter in Asyl: Fragment." *Merkur* 24 (1970): 1163f.
"Protest." *Theater heute* 13 (Sept. 1972): 14.
"Der Ignorant und der Wahnsinnige." *Theater heute* 13 (Sept. 1972): 34–47.
"Die Jagdgesellschaft." *Spectaculum* 20 (1974): 15–79.
"Die Macht der Gewohnheit." *Theater heute* 15 (Sept. 1974): 37–52.
"Die Komödie der Eitelkeit." *Die Zeit,* 27 Feb. 1976: 55.

"Der deutsche Mittagstisch: Eine Tragödie für ein Burgtheatergastspiel in Deutschland." *Die Zeit*, 29 Dec. 1978: 33.
"Der Weltverbesserer." *Theater* (1978): 88–102.
"Was Österreich nicht lesen soll: Die Kleinbürger auf der Heuchelleiter." *Die Zeit*, 17 Feb. 1978: 40.
"Der doppelte Herr Bernhard." *Die Zeit*, 31 Aug. 1979: 43f.
"Zu meinem Austritt." *Frankfurter Allgemeine Zeitung*, 7 Dec. 1979: 25.
"Vor dem Ruhestand: Eine Komödie von deutscher Seele." *Theater heute* 19 (Aug. 1979): 33–49.
"A Doda: Für zwei Schauspielerinnen und eine Landstraβe." *Die Zeit*, 12 Dec. 1980: 40.
"Der pensionierte Salonsozialist." *Profil*, 26 Jan. 1981: 5–9.
"Alles oder nichts: Ein deutscher Akt." *Theater heute* 22 (May 1981): 5–9.
"Am Ziel." *Theater heute* 22 (Oct. 1981): 35–53.
"Verfolgungswahn?" *Die Zeit*, 11 Jan. 1982: 32.
"Goethe schtirbt." *Die Zeit*, 19 Mar. 1982: 41f.
"Montaigne: Eine Erzählung in 22 Fortsetzungen." *Die Zeit*, 8 Oct. 1982: 1–22.
"Der Schein trügt." *Spectaculum* 39 (1984): 17–77.
"Vranitzky: Eine Erwiderung." *Die Presse*, 13 Sept. 1985.
"Claus Peymann verläβt Bochum und geht als Burgtheaterdirektor nach Wien." *Die Zeit*, 9 May 1986: 51.
"Claus Peymann kauft sich eine Hose und geht mit mir essen." *Theater* 1986: 6–10.
"Claus Peymann und Hermann Beil auf der Sulzwiese." *Die Zeit*, 11 Sept. 1987: 53–54.
"Einfach kompliziert." *Spectaculum* 46 (1988): 7–42.
"Mein glückliches Österreich." *Die Zeit*, 11 Mar. 1988: 75.
"Zwei Briefe an Claus Peymann." *Die Zeit*, 3 Mar. 1989: 14.

INTERVIEWS

"Je remplis le vide avec des phrases." *Nouvelles littéraires*, 22–29 June 1978: 18.
"Thomas Bernhard." André Müller, *Entblöβungen*. Munich: Goldmann, 1979. 59–102.
"Ich könnte auf dem Papier jemand umbringen." *Der Spiegel*, 23 June 1980: 172–82.
"Ansichten eines unverbesserlichen Weltverbesserers." *Stern*, 4 June 1981: 160–62.
"Aveux et paradoxes de Thomas Bernhard." *Le Monde*, 7 Jan. 1983: 15.
"Ich behaupte nicht, mit der Welt gehe es schlechter: Aus einem Gespräch mit Thomas Bernhard." *Frankfurter Allgemeine Zeitung*, 24 Feb. 1983: 23.
" 'Es ist eh alles positiv.' Thomas Bernhard über seine Bücher, seine Feinde und sich selbst." *Die Presse* 22/23 Sept. 1984. "Spektrum" supplement.
"Von einer Katastrophe in die andere." *Süddeutsche Zeitung*, 17/18 Jan. 1987: 169–70.

BIBLIOGRAPHY

"Eine groteske Phantomedebatte." *Profil,* 17 Oct. 1988.
Aus Gesprächen mit Thomas Bernhard. Ed. Kurt Hofmann. Vienna: Löcker, 1988.
"Letzte Worte aus der Einsamkeit." *Der Spiegel,* 29 Jan. 1990: 160–70.

Critical Works

BIBLIOGRAPHIES

Carpenter, Charles A. *Modern Drama Scholarship and Criticism 1966–1980: An International Bibliography.* Toronto: University of Toronto Press, 1986. 318.
Daviau, Donald. "The Reception of Thomas Bernhard in the United States." *Modern Austrian Literature* 21, 3/4 (1988): 267–76. A useful essay and helpful bibliography.
Dittmar, Jens. *Thomas Bernhard Werkgeschichte.* 2d rev. ed. Frankfurt am Main: Suhrkamp, 1990. A thorough guide to works by and about Thomas Bernhard. Includes a wide range of excerpts of reviews and essays. Indispensable.
Sorg, Bernhard, and Michael Töteberg. "Thomas Bernhard." *Kritisches Lexikon zur deutschsprachigen Gegenwartsliteratur.* Ed. Heinz Ludwig Arnold. Munich: Edition Text + Kritik, 1978ff. Not as useful as Dittmar.

BOOKS

Botond, Anneliese, ed. *Über Thomas Bernhard.* Frankfurt am Main: Suhrkamp, 1970. A collection of the early responses to Bernhard, including essays by Handke and Zuckmayer.
Calandra, Denis. *New German Dramatists.* New York: Grove, 1983. 139–61. Briefly sets Bernhard into the larger perspective of contemporary German drama.
Craft, Robert. "Comedian of Horror." *New York Review of Books,* 27 Sept. 1990: 40–48.
Endres, Ria. *Am Ende angekommen: Dargestellt am wahnhaften Dunkel der Männerporträts des Thomas Bernhard.* Frankfurt am Main: Fischer, 1980. A hostile interpretation from the viewpoint of feminism.
Fischer, Bernhard. *"Gehen" von Thomas Bernhard: Eine Studie zum Problem der Moderne.* Bonner Arbeiten zur deutschen Literatur 43. Bonn: Bouvier, 1985. A philosophically schooled reading of the short novel *Gehen.*
Gamper, Herbert. *Thomas Bernhard.* Munich: Deutscher Taschenbuch Verlag, 1977. A short survey of the fiction and drama into the mid-1970s.
Gößling, Andreas. *Thomas Bernhards frühe Prosakunst.* Berlin: de Gruyter, 1987. A detailed study of *Frost, Gargoyles,* and *Correction* with emphasis on themes of selfhood and consciousness. Operates on the not very persuasive premise that the later works are inferior.

Hervé, Lenormand, and Werner Wögerbauer, eds. *Thomas Bernhard*. Nantes: Arcane 17, 1987. Essays on Bernhard from France.
Caroline Markolin, *Die Großväter sind die Lehrer: Johannes Freumbichler und sein Enkel Thomas Bernhard*. Salzburg: Otto Müller, 1988. Focuses attention on the grandfather and helps to fill out the picture of Bernhard's youth.
Meyerhofer, Nicholas J. *Thomas Bernhard*. Köpfe des 20. Jahrhunderts, 104. Berlin: Colloquium, 1985. Short survey of Bernhard's drama and fiction into the mid-1980s.
Pittertschatscher, Alfred, ed. *Literarisches Kolloquium Linz '84: Thomas Bernhard*. Schriftenreihe literarisches Kolloquium Linz 1. Linz: Land Oberösterreich, 1985. Proceedings of a symposium, including an essay by Bernhard's director Peymann.
Schmidt-Dengler, Wendelin. *Der Übertreibungskünstler: Studien zu Thomas Bernhard*. 2d rev. ed. Vienna: Sonderzahl, 1989. A collection of nine diverse essays by an informed and informing Austrian observer.
Schmidt-Dengler, Wendelin, and Martin Huber, eds. *Statt Bernhard: Über Misanthropie im Werk Thomas Bernhards*. Vienna: Edition S, 1987. Eight essays by different critics emphasizing Bernhard's troubled relationship to Austria.
Sorg, Bernhard. *Thomas Bernhard*. Autorenbücher 7. Munich: Beck, 1977. A short survey.

ARTICLES: FICTION

Améry, Jean. "Morbus Austriacus." *Merkur* 30 (1976): 91–96; "Atemnot," *Merkur* 32 (1978): 947–49. Reviews of *The Cause*, *Breath*, and *Correction* by an Austrian expatriate.
Anderson, Mark. "Notes on Thomas Bernhard." *Raritan* 7 (1987): 81–96.
Birkerts, Sven. "Thomas Bernhard." *An Artificial Wilderness*. New York: Morrow, 1987. 77–84.
Blöcker, Günter. "Wie Existenznot durch Sprachnot glaubwürdig wird." *Merkur* 24 (Dec. 1970): 1181–87. Penetrating discussion of Bernhard and language occasioned by the Büchner Prize.
Craig, D. A. "The Novels of Thomas Bernhard: A Report." *German Life and Letters* 25 (1972): 343–53.
Dahlhaus, Carl. "Lauter Untergeher: Der Anti-Psycholog Thomas Bernhard." *Die Zeit*, 13 Jan. 1984, 36.
Demetz, Peter. "Thomas Bernhard: The Dark Side of Life." *After the Fires: Recent Writing in the Germanies, Switzerland, and Austria*. New York: Harcourt, Brace Jovanovich, 1986. 199–212. An important survey of German-language literary life since 1945 that helps clarify Bernhard's place in the tradition.
Dierick, A. P. "Thomas Bernhard's Austrian Neurosis." *Modern Austrian Literature* 12/1 (1979): 73–93.
Donnenberg, Josef. "Thomas Bernhard und Österreich." *Österreich in Geschichte und Gegenwart* 14 (1970): 237–51.

Eben, Michael C. "Thomas Bernhard's *Frost*: Early Indications of an Austrian Demise." *Neophilologus* 69 (1985): 590–603.
Falkenberg, Betty. "Thomas Bernhard: An Introduction." *Partisan Review* 47 (1980): 269–77.
Fetz, Gerald. "Thomas Bernhard and the 'Modern Novel.'" *The Modern German Novel*. Ed. Keith Bullivant. Leamington Spa, UK: Berg, 1987.
———. "Thomas Bernhard und die österreichische Tradition." *Österreichische Gegenwart*. Ed. Wolfgang Paulsen. Bern: Francke, 1980. 189–205.
Godwin-Jones, Robert. "The Terrible Idyll: Thomas Bernhard's *Das Kalkwerk*." *Germanic Notes* 13 (1982): 8–10.
Ingen, Ferdinand van. "Denk-Übungen: Zum Prosawerk Thomas Bernhards." *Studien zur österreichischen Erzählliteratur der Gegenwart*. Ed. Herbert Zeman. *Amsterdamer Beiträge zur neueren Germanistik* 14 (1982): 37–86.
Kafitz, Dieter. "Die Problematisierung des individualistischen Menschenbildes im deutschsprachigen Theater der Gegenwart." *Basis* 10 (1980): 93–126.
Kralicek, Wolfgang. "Sein Wille geschehe: Thomas Bernhards letzter Text sorgt posthum für Erregung." (Vienna) *Wochenpresse*, 24 Feb. 1989: 42–43. A journalist's account of the flap created by Bernhard's will.
Latimer, Renate. "Thomas Bernhard's Image of Woman." *Germanic Notes* 8 (1977): 25–27.
Lüdke, Martin, "Ein 'Ich' in der Bewegung stillgestellt: Wegmarken der Bernhardschen Autobiographie." *Merkur* 35 (1981): 1175–83. An especially perceptive essay on Bernhard's memoirs.
Mauch, Gudrun. "Thomas Bernhards Biographie des Schmerzes." *Modern Austrian Literature* 13 (1980): 91–110.
———. "Thomas Bernhards Roman *Korrektur*." *Amsterdamer Beiträge zur Germanistik* 14 (1982): 87–106.
Mayer, Hans. "Thomas Bernhard." *Die unerwünschte Literatur: Deutsche Schriftsteller und Bücher 1968–1985*. Vol. 2. Berlin: Siedler, 1989. 151–57.
Rossbacher, Karlheinz. "Thomas Bernhard: *Das Kalkwerk*." *Deutsche Romane des 20. Jahrhunderts*. Ed. Paul Michael Lützeler. Königstein: Athenäum, 1983.
Schlaes, Amity. "Thomas Bernhard and the German Literary Scene." *The New Criterion* 5 (Jan. 1982): 26–32.
Schödel, Helmut. "Wenn ihr nicht brav seid, kommt der Bernhard: Ohlsdorf nach dem Tod des Dichters." *Die Zeit*, 11 Aug. 1989: 15–16.
Seydel, Bernd. *Die Vernunft der Winterkälte: Gleichgültigkeit als Equilibrismus im Werk Thomas Bernhards*. Epistemata, Reihe Literaturwissenschaft 22. Würzburg: Königshausen + Neumann, 1986.
Škreb, Zdenko. "Weltbild und Form bei Thomas Bernhard." *Literatur aus Österreich, österreichische Literatur*. Ed. Karl Konrad Polheim. Bonn: Bouvier, 1981. 145–66.

Thomas, Noel. "The Structure of a Nightmare: Autobiography and Art in Thomas Bernhard's *Der Keller*." *Quinqereme* 6 (1983): 155–66.
Thorpe, Kathleen. "The Autobiographical Works of Thomas Bernhard." *Acta Germanica* 13 (1980): 189–200.
Updike, John. "Ungreat Lives." *The New Yorker*, 4 Feb. 1985: 97–101; "Studies in Post-Hitlerian Self-condemnation in Germany and Austria." *The New Yorker*, 9 Oct. 1989, 132–36. Acute reflections on *Wittgenstein's Nephew*.
Weber, Albrecht. "Wittgensteins Gestalt und Theorie und ihre Wirkung im Werk Thomas Bernhards." *Österreich in Geschichte und Literatur* 25 (1981): 86–104.
Weiss, Walter. "Thomas Bernhard–Franz Kafka." *London German Studies* 2 (1983): 184–98.
Wiese, Benno von. "Thomas Bernhard." *Otium et Negotium*. Ed. Folke Sandgren. Stockholm: Kungl, 1972. 632–46.

ARTICLES: DRAMA

Barthofer, Arnold. "Vorliebe für die Kömodie: Todesangst. Anmerkungen zum Kömodienbegriff bei Thomas Bernhard." *Vierteljahresschrift des Adalbert-Stifter-Instituts* 31 (1982): 77–100.
———. "King Lear in Dinkelsbühl: Historisch-biographisches zu Thomas Bernhards Theaterstück *Minetti*." *Maske und Kothurn* 23 (1977): 158–72.
———. "The Plays of Thomas Bernhard—A Report." *Modern Austrian Literature* 11/1 (1978): 21–48.
Becker, Peter von. "Bei Bernhard: eine Geschichte in 15 Episoden." *Theater heute* 19, supplement 1977/78, (1978): 80–87; "Die Unvernünftigen sterben nicht aus: Über Bernhards *Vor dem Ruhestand*." *Theater heute* 20 (1979): 4–11. Two characteristic essays from one of the influential Swiss theater journal's principal reviewers; *Theater heute* was one of the strong supporters of Bernhard's theater.
Demet, Michel. "Le Théâtre de Thomas Bernhard." *Etudes germaniques* 31 (1976): 58–66.
Dermutz, Klaus. "Rücksichtslosigkeit und Charme: Ein Gespräch mit Bernhard Minetti kurz vor Thomas Bernhards Tod." *Theater* 1989: 29–30.
Ehrig, Heinz. "Probleme des Absurden: Vergleichende Bemerkungen zu Bernhard und Beckett." *Wirkendes Wort* 29 (1978): 44–64.
Eisner, Nicholas. "Theatertheater/Theaterspiele: The Plays of Thomas Bernhard." *Modern Drama* 30 (1987): 104–14.
Esslin, Martin. "A Drama of Disease and Derision: The Plays of Thomas Bernhard." *Modern Drama* 23 (1981): 367–84; "Beckett and Bernhard: A Comparison." *Modern Austrian Literature* 18 (1985): 67–78; "Contemporary Austrian Playwrights." *Performing Arts Journal* 3 (1978): 93–98. Three basic and useful essays by a seasoned observer of the modern German stage.

Federico, Joseph. "Millenarianism, Legitimation, and the National Socialist Universe of Thomas Bernhard's *Vor dem Ruhestand*." *Germanic Review* 59 (1984): 142–48.

Görner, Rüdiger. "Thomas Bernhard." *A Radical Stage*. Ed. W. G. Sebald. Oxford: Berg, 1988. 161–73.

Groβklaus, Götz. "Österreichische Mythen: Zu zwei Filmen von Bernhard und Handke." *Lili* 29 (1978): 40–62.

Gross, Robert, Jr. "The Perils of Performance in Thomas Bernhard's *Der Ignorant und der Wahnsinnige*." *Modern Drama* 23 (1981): 385–92.

Hannemann, Bruno. "Satirisches Psychogramm der Mächtigen: Zur Kunst der Provokation in Thomas Bernhards *Der Präsident*." *Maske und Kothurn* 23 (1977): 147–58.

———. "Totentanz der Marionetten: Monotonie und Manier bei Thomas Bernhard." *Modern Austrian Literature* 13 (1980): 123–50.

———. "Vernunft und Irrfahrt: Zu Thomas Bernhards Komödie *Immanuel Kant*." *Maske und Kothurn* 27 (1981): 346–59.

Henrichs, Benjamin. "Heldenplatz, Die Schlacht ums Wiener Burgtheater." *Die Zeit*, 21 Oct. 1988: 67–68.

———. "Ein Toter wird ermordet: *Elisabeth II*, die letzte Thomas Bernhard Uraufführung." *Die Zeit*, 10 Nov. 1989: 80.

Honegger, Gitta. "How German Is It? Thomas Bernhard at the Guthrie." *Performing Arts Journal* 6 (1981): 1–17; "Wittgenstein's Children: The Writings of Thomas Bernhard." *Theater* 15 (1983): 58–62; "Acoustic Masks: Strategies of Language in the Theater of Canetti, Bernhard, and Handke." *Modern Austrian Literature* 18 (1985): 57–66. Commentaries of a Viennese-born American director, including remarks on the failed American production of *Eve of Retirement*. Honegger, who has translated most of the Bernhard dramas that are available in English, also knew the writer personally.

May, Terrill. "Thomas Bernhard's *Der Ignorant und der Wahnsinnige*: An Analysis of Dramatic Style." *Modern Language Studies* 9 (1978/79): 60–72.

Melchinger, Siegfried. "Das Material ist die Wahrheit der Welt: *Die Jagdgesellschaft*." *Theater heute* 15 (1974): 8–9.

Mennemeier, Franz. "Nachhall des absurden Dramas: Thomas Bernhard." *Modernes deutsches Drama: Kritiken und Charakteristiken*. Vol. 2. Ed. F. Mennemeier. Munich: Fink, 1975. 307–320.

Merschmeier, Michael. "Heldenspatz: Bernhards *Heldenplatz* am Wiener Burgtheater." *Theater heute* 29 (1988): 1ff.

Michaelis, Rolf. "Mein Salzburg—eine Todesstadt: Das Neueste vom Dauerkrach Thomas Bernhards mit den Salzburger Festspielen." *Die Zeit*, 29 Aug. 1975: 33.

Strauβ, Botho. "Komödie aus Todesangst: Thomas Bernhard *Ein Fest für Boris* in Berlin." *Theater heute* 11 (1970): 30–32. A review of Bernhard's first play by one of Germany's most celebrated contemporary playwrights.

BIBLIOGRAPHY

SPECIAL ISSUES OF JOURNALS

Modern Austrian Literature 21, 3/4 (1988).
Text und Kontext 14 (1987).
Text + Kritik 43 (1974).

Index

Adorno, Theodor, 17
allegory, 31, 24
Améry, Jean, 80–83
Amras, 9, 21–22, 34–35, 37
anti-semitism, 66, 79–83
Artaud, Antonin, 15; Theater of Cruelty, 20
Auerbach, Erich, 32
Auslöchung, 25, 65–70
Austria, 2, 7, 11–15, 21–22, 47, 54, 59; cultural politics in, 11–12, 22, 27 n.3, 55; cultural identity of, 11–14, 74–75; founding of the Second Republic, 11; and Nazism, 13, 22, 79–83; symbolized as female character, 61, 66–68
Austrian State Prize for Literature, 45, 48
authenticity, xi, 35; Bernhard's rejection of, 6–7; in drama and fiction, 29–30
autonomy, theme of, 7

Bachmann, Ingeborg, 67
Bacon, Francis, 20
Bernhard, Anna, 57 n.6
Bernhard, Herta. See Fabjan, Herta
Bernhard, Thomas: anarchism of, 49, 52–54, 79, 82; attitude toward language, 14, 30–31, 51, 67–68; attitude toward nature, 19, 23–24, 69; attitude toward theater, 71; Catholicism of, 6–7, 14, 49; characteristic themes of, 2, 4, 6–7, 18–19, 21–24, 65–66; critique of mystifications, xii, 6–7, 9, 17, 49–50, 55–56, 63–64, 70, 76; death of, 2, 43, 83; difficult to interview, 43–44; and disease, 8–9, 18–20, 52–56, 60; ethical attitude of, xii, 3–4, 7–8, 23, 65–66, 69–70, 79, 82; humor of, 4, 17, 25–26, 45, 61; and irony, 8, 17–18, 33; life of, 8–9, 14–15, 47–56; literary prizes of, 56–57 n.2; literary technique of, 1, 29–31, compared to Kafka's, 31–33; misanthropy of, 17, 43–44, 54 (*see also* misogyny); mother of, 8–9, 53–54, 56; and music, 1, 52, 56; opposition to theories, 51–52; pessimism of, 7–9, 24, 47, 59, 79; and philosophy, xiii, 17, 26, 51; political attitudes of, 2, 3, 6, 43, 79; public image of, 43–46, 49; schooling of, 49–51; style of, 1–2, 9, 31–33, 71–72; unfinished works, 46, 71
Die Berühmten, 73.
The Big Names. See Die Berühmten
Böll, Heinrich, 11, 46
Bosch, Hieronymus, 20, 24
Breath, 52–53
Brecht, Bertolt, 11
Breughel, Jan, 20
Broch, Hermann, xiii, 11, 13, 23
Burgtheater, 44, 72, 79

Camus, Albert, 4
Canetti, Elias, 3, 11, 46
Catholicism, 6, 14, 29, 50, 74
Celan, Paul, 11
The Cellar, 50–51
Cervantes, Miguel de, 17
The Cheap-Eaters, 62
A Child, 48
Concrete, 61–62
Conrad, Joseph, *Heart of Darkness,* 15
Correction, 1, 31, 36–41, 63, 67, 81; and *Old Masters,* 60–61

death: theme of, 4, 6–7, 9–10, 38, 40, 41, 62–70; and forgetting, 20, 25
Dene, Kirsten, 72
disease, metaphor of, 19–20, 65–66
Dostoyevsky, Fyodor, 19; *The Demons,* 18, 56

INDEX

Einfach kompliziert, 72
Elisabeth II, 71, 73
Enzensberger, Hans Magnus, 29
Eve of Retirement, 34, 67, 76–79
existentialism, 4–5

Fabjan, Emil, 57 n.6
Fabjan, Herta, 8–9, 56; death of, 53–54
family: symbol of Austrian nation, 21–22, 33, 39, 66–70
Faulkner, William, 67
Filbinger, Hans Karl, 76–77
The Force of Habit, 62, 75–76
forgetting, theme of, 16, 20, 25, 49–50, 65, 79–83
Freud, Sigmund, 21, 23, 64
Freumbichler, Johannes, 15, 43, 48–49; death of, 52–53
Frost, 15–25, 35, 52, 67

Ganz, Bruno, 71
Gargoyles, 1, 21, 24–26, 36, 52
Gathering Evidence, 47–56
German Academy of Language and Literature, 45–46, 54, 59
Gödel, Kurt, 23
Going Under. See *Der Untergeher.*
Gould, Glenn, 6, 62–63
Grass, Günter, 11
Graz Writers' Collective, 13
Grillparzer, Franz, 45
Grillparzer Prize, 45

Handke, Peter, 13; *Insulting the Audience,* 44
Hašek, Jaroslav, 17
Heerdegen, Edith, 71
Heidegger, Martin, 40, 61
Heldenplatz, 9, 79–83
history, theme of: xii, 3, 7, 12, 22–23, 64–70, 76; and sister figure, 38, 78–79
Histrionics, 73
Hochhuth, Rolf, 29; *The Lawyers,* 77
Hofmannsthal, Hugo von, 13, 74
humor, 4–5, 17, 24–26, 61
The Hunting Party, 72

The Ingnoramus and the Madman. See *Der Ignorant und der Wahnsinnige*
Der Ignorant und der Wahnsinnige, 73
incest, theme of: 19, 22, 24, 34–36; as symbol, 35, 78
An Indication of the Cause, 49, 81
intellectual fanaticism, 29, 33, 36, 49, 67; and Johannes Freumbichler, 48–50
In the Cold, 53

Ja, 61
Joyce, James, 17, 32

Kafka, Franz, xiii, 8, 13, 18, 23, 41; *The Castle,* 15; narrative technique of, 31–33; theme of truth, 51
Kant, Immanuel, 64
Kipphardt, Heinar, 29
Koestler, Arthur, 11
Kraus, Karl, 14
Kreisky, Bruno, 3
Kundera, Milan, 5

Lampersberg, Gerhard, 55
Leyen, Prince Ferdinand von der, 81
The Lime Works, 1, 4, 29–36, 62

Maier, Hans, 80. See also Améry, Jean
Mann, Thomas, xiii; *The Magic Mountain,* 15; and theme of disease, 19–20, 23
Mauthner, Fritz, 14
Mendelssohn-Bartholdy, Felix, 6, 62
Minetti, Bernhard, 71–72
misogyny, 17, 35, 37
Montaigne, Michel de, 47
morality, theme of: 3, 7–8; and anarchy, 69–70, 79
Moscow Declaration, 11
Musil, Robert, xiii, 7, 11, 13, 23; *The Man Without Qualities,* 32–34

Nazism, 3, 6, 11, 49–50, 54, 66–70, 79–83
Neufundland, 46
Newfoundland. See *Neufundland*
Nietzsche, Friedrich, xiv, 2, 7; and high art, 63–64
Novalis, 19

INDEX

Obliteration. See Auslöschung
Old Masters, 22–23, 27 n.2, 40, 60–65
Ortega y Gasset, José, 69

A Party for Boris, 17, 73
Pascal, Blaise, xiii, 16
Percy, Walker, 18
perfection, as theme, 6, 29, 31–32, 63; in *Correction*, 39; in *Old Masters*, 64
Peymann, Claus, 71, 72, 76; in Stuttgart, 75–77; in Vienna, 79–83
Playing Cards. See Watten
plot, 5, 19, 48
pride, theme of, 6, 36. *See also* intellectual fanaticism
psychoanalysis, 3, 32
psychological novel, 24, 32

Rabelais, François, 17
Radio Austria, 14
redemption, theme of, 40, 56, 76. *See also* transcendence
Reinhardt, Max, 74
Rilke, Rainer Maria, 13
Ritter, Ilse, 72
Ritter, Dene, Voss, 72
Roth, Joseph, 11

Salzburg, 2, 14, 49–51, 53, 74
Salzburg Festival, 49, 73–75
satire, xii, 3, 16–18, 55, 69–70, 78
Scheel, Walter, 46
Schönberg, Arnold, 23
Schopenhauer, Arthur, 25–26
Der Schweinehüter, 14
self, 5, 31–32, 36, 51, 53–54, 56; in *Correction*, 36; in *The Lime Works*, 33–34; in *Auslöschung*, 68
sex, 5, 23–24, 35. *See also* incest
Shakespeare, William, 64
Simply Complicated. See Einfach kompliziert
sister: as key figure, 21, 34, 36–41, 60–61, 63
Sisyphus, 4
Soyfer, Jura, 11
suicide, 5–6, 11, 36–37, 39–40, 63

Sprachskepsis, 14; and Bernhard's technique, 30–32
Stifter, Adalbert, 61
Der Stimmenimitator, 5
Strauss, Richard, 74
surrealism, 13–14
Swift, Jonathan, xii, 2, 4; *Gulliver's Travels*, 17–19
The Swineherd. See Der Schweinehüter

Trakl, Georg, 18, 56
theater: and language, 72; Bernhard's alleged contempt for, 71
transcendence, theme of, 4–5, 18, 40–41, 60–65, 75–76
Twain, Mark, 17

Ungenach, 21–22
Der Untergeher, 62–64

Vergangenheitsbewältigung, 69
Viennese Academy of Sciences, 45
The Voice Mimic. See Der Stimmenimitator
Voss, Gert, 72

Waldheim, Kurt, 12, 27n. 2, 77, 81–82
Watten, 9
Weigel, Hans, 15
Weiss, Ernst, 11
Weiss, Peter, 29
Wessely, Paula, 71
Wiener Gruppe, 12
wildernness, metaphor of, 19, 39
Wittgenstein, Ludwig, xii, 6, 7, 23; as model for Roithamer, 36
Wittgenstein's Nephew, xi, 19, 45
women: as symbolic image, 16–17, 34–39, 57 n.7. *See also* sister *and* misogyny
Woodcutters, 15, 54

Yes. See Ja

Zuckerstätter, Alois, 8, 48
Zuckmayer, Carl, 15, 27 n.13
Zweig, Stefan, 15

OHIO